# THE OWL PEN

# THE
# OWL PEN

## Kenneth McNeill Wells

Woodcuts by
## Lucille Oille

Stoddart

Published in 1995 by
Stoddart Publishing Co. Limited
34 Lesmill Road
Toronto, Canada
M3B 2T6
Tel. (416) 445-3333
Fax (416) 445-5967

Stoddart Books are available for bulk purchase for sales promotions, premiums, fundraising, and seminars. For details, contact the Special Sales Department at the above address.

Hardcover edition published in 1947 by
J. M. Dent & Sons (Canada) Limited

Canadian Cataloguing in Publication Data

Wells, Kenneth McNeill, 1905–1988
The owl pen

ISBN 0-7737-5746-5

1. Wells, Kenneth McNeill, 1905–1988 – Anecdotes.
2. Oille, Lucille – Anecdotes.  3. Country life –
Ontario – Medonte (Township) – Anecdotes.
I. Oille, Lucille.   II. Title

S522.C2W45  1995      630'.9713'17      C95-931043-6

Cover Design: Tannice Goddard
Printed and bound in Canada

*Stoddart Publishing gratefully acknowledges the support of the Canada Council, the Ontario Ministry of Culture, Tourism, and Recreation, Ontario Arts Council, and Ontario Publishing Centre in the development of writing and publishing in Canada.*

*This book is dedicated to*
*Lucy's Parents*
*Dr. and Mrs. John Allen Oille*
*and to*
*The Memory of My Father*
*John Page Wells*

# ACKNOWLEDGEMENTS

Mr. C. H. J. Snider, associate editor of the *Evening Telegram*, Toronto, thought that the story of Owl Pen would look well as a series of articles in the Saturday editions of that journal. Mr. A.W. J. Buckland, news editor, with his sympathetic handling of my manuscript, made sure that it did. Now the *Evening Telegram*, through its managing editor, Mr. C.O. Knowles, C.B.E., has given its permission for me to use the material appearing first in its columns to make this book.

In this instance, to say "thank you" is to say little and mean much.

*Kenneth McNeill Wells, 1947*


My thanks to Jamie Hunter, Barb Robillard, Pat Souter, and Stephen McCanse, for their help in bringing this book back to the public through Stoddart Publishing.

*Lucille (Oille) Wells, 1995*

# CONTENTS

# PART 1

## Such Simple Folk

*"I never had any other desire so strong, and so like to covetousness, as that one which I have had always, that I might be master at last of a small house and large garden, with very moderate conveniences joined to them ..."*

ABRAHAM COWLEY, 1666

# 1

### *We Find an Abandoned House*

IN THE TOWNSHIP OF MEDONTE, BETWEEN THE MOON-
stone and the Coldwater valleys, is a flat-topped hill. Small
farms, and smaller woodlands, dapple its sides. Trout-
haunted streams wash its base. A single road crosses it,
running with prim straightness past gray rail fences and a
magnificent dry stone wall, past venerable maple trees, and
cloud-fingering elms. The road runs on past a field that is
notable now only for the fact that in its exact centre there
stands, for no apparent reason at all, a lonely wooden pump.

The pump had a reason for being when Lucy and I first
came upon it. Then it was part of all that was left of a
pioneer homestead. Then it stood in the midst of a dying
orchard, at the foot of a ruined garden, with a roofless root
cellar beside it, with the poor skeleton of a picket fence

3

around it, and in front of it, between it and the road, the leaning wreck of a house.

It was a sad old house, woe-begone, beaten, like a fine old lady fallen on evil days. Bees hummed in the clover blossoms. Birds whistled in the locust trees. Everywhere there was life, the bustle, aroma, and music of life, the keenness and colour of summer living. Only the old house seemed oblivious to it all. Its sagging room seemed hunched in misery.

"The poor old thing!" said Lucy.

"Let's give it a call," said I.

We opened the drunken road gate, and walked into the ruined garden. Old-fashioned flowers struggled wanly with twitch grass and buttercups. Old-fashioned roses shared a tumbled fence corner with burdocks and barbed wire. On what had once been a gravelled path a broken tea cup glistened in the sun. A garter snake crawled unhurriedly away from our advancing feet into a clump of ragweed, and an unseen chipmunk cursed us and told us to get out.

The old house stared with blind eyes out its glassless windows as we approached. The front door hung giddily over grass-grown wreckage that had once been wooden steps. Behind it, in the dark hall, we could see, dimly, a tangle of broken furniture, old lumber, and fence posts. There was a fungi-spotted organ, and a chair with three mossy legs. A long-dead bird sprawled on a window sill.

We climbed into the house, past the little feathered mummy, to a scene of utter desolation. Rot was everywhere. Rain-stained plaster hung in hair-held festoons from walls and ceilings. Looking up through an oblong chasm that had once held a staircase, we saw daylight glimmering fitfully through broken roof boards. The place stunk of decay, and yet as we walked through it, opening small latched doors of time-coloured pine, passing from one small room to another, we felt that the old house had been, and somehow still was, a kindly sort of house.

"The old place has been murdered," sighed Lucy.

"You can say that again," boomed a voice behind us.

It was as though the house itself had spoken. Lucy squeaked. I dropped my pipe. We turned, with popping mouths and bulging eyes, to find a gray-haired farmer leaning, with a quizzical grin, on the window sill behind us.

"Quite a wreck, ain't it?" he continued, his eyes twinkling with appreciation of our discomfiture. "Was the first house ever built on this concession line, cut out of the bush and put up by two brothers, George and Jim Coulson, back in 1830. People still talk about what those fellows could do with an axe. Shame to see the old place go to pieces like this . . . " He shrugged, and spat tobacco juice at the dead bird. "Still, it's made of pine, and pine is never so rotten it won't make a fire."

"A fire!" I exclaimed.

"Sure," returned the farmer. "Burning is all it's good for now, more's the pity. They don't grow timbers to-day like them this house is made of. It ain't the frame shack you might think. Around at the back, where the woodshed has fallen away, where there ain't any clapboard, you can see the finest, and biggest, white pine timbers man ever put an eye on. Three feet wide some of them are, and cut flat to a chalk line with adze and broad axe. Smooth as mill work . . . " He paused to bite with yellow teeth into a black plug of chewing tobacco. "Even after all these years, an' all this rot, everything still fits like it was made yesterday." He chewed awhile. "Only yesterday they couldn't hew like this house was hewed. Go 'round and take a look."

Lucy and I did as we were told. After all, we were trespassers, and the old man might be the owner. We humoured him. We climbed back out of the house, through the window, and went around to where a pile of rotting boards and shingles told of a shed that had been. We took a look, and gasped, and looked again. The biggest white pine timbers that we had ever seen lay piled into a wall in front of us. Artists with axes had hewn them out of trees, the like of which do not now grow on this earth. They glowed softly in the sunlight, like huge hammered slabs of ancient silver.

Somehow, as Lucy and I stood there staring at the unexpected beauty a collapsing woodshed and a garrulous old man had discovered to us, the mists of history crept over Stone Wall Hill. The parent seeds of those mighty sticks had sprouted generations before white men dreamed that over the western ocean was a strange, new world. As saplings they had heard the whine of the red man's hunting arrow. For all we knew they had seen Champlain. They had heard the howling of savage warriors, and had witnessed the blood-wet agony of pillage and massacre. As great trees towering in a sombre forest, they had seen the first settlers tramping through the wilderness that was Medonte. They had felt the bite of a pioneer's axe.

As timbers in the old house they had seen an ancient Indian trail grow into a tote road, into the white gravelled artery of a township. They had seen the dog-sleigh of the Indian give way to the ox-drawn cart of the settler, to a horse-drawn wagon, to a motor car. They had seen cattle and sheep crowd out the deer. They had seen the lynx and the martin give way to the prowling barnyard cat. They had seen a people die and a nation grow. The years had passed over them and their day was done.

"I suppose burning is all the old place is good for now," I agreed, unhappily.

I heard a snort beside me.

"We're going to live in this house," said Lucy.

The oracle had spoken.

# 2

## *We Stumble Into Eden*

LUCY AND I BOUGHT THE OLD GRAY HOUSE ON STONE WALL Hill for fifteen dollars. It was a cash deal. We bought the house for the price of a pair of boots, but not the land it stood on. Light-heartedly we promised that within six weeks we would move it from its ancient site, dig up the old foundations, burn or bury rubbish and wreckage, and leave all fit for ploughing. The township buzzed with the tale of our folly. The concession telephone lines shook with the laughter of the gossiping farm folk. It was rumoured that we had no land to which we could move our purchase. It was rumoured that we were shopping for land, and could find none to suit us. It was rumoured that our time limit was running out. The rumours were true.

Lucy and I scrabbled through the countryside, like hungry chickens through a straw pile, looking for four or five acres —just four or five acres—on which to place our home to be. All we wanted was a bit of creek and a waterfall, some nice old trees, a chunk of garden land, range for some chickens, pasture for some goats, and room for a bee-yard and orchard. Lucy thought that there should be wild flowers on the creek bank, and water-cress in the shallows. I was equally insistent that there should be eight-inch trout in the deeper pools.

When we began our search, we felt that we were reasonably modest in our requirements. It was with something approaching hurt surprise that we learned that farmers do

not ordinarily jump at the chance of selling five-acre pieces
out of their farms. As our search wore on, we awoke to
the fact that our task was not only to find land that pleased
us. It was to find land that pleased us that was owned by a
farmer who would sell at a price we could afford to pay.
We began to think that we were biting at the moon. The
site we sought seemed out of this world.

"Try Eden," suggested a friend.

We did not think him funny, perhaps because in our
hearts we knew that it was something out of Eden for which
we were looking. And there seemed little chance of finding it in Medonte. Compromise was indicated. We pared
our requirements to what we considered a bare minimum.
The search went on. I found a place I thought, reluctantly,
would do. Lucy screamed that it would not. She found a
place that she thought might just satisfy us. I howled my
refusal to be found dead on it.

Once, success seemed ours. We stood in a lawyer's office,
our cheque books trembling with eagerness, on the point
of purchasing a bit of land that even Adam might have
liked, when fate stepped in with a whisper. In the springtime, our proposed building site was four feet under water.
We walked out of that deal with our mad hairs standing
straight up. What sort of fools did people think we were?
What sort of fools were we?

Day after day, night after night, we drove our dusty
little car up and down the concession lines of Medonte.
Night after night, we laid ourselves down to sleep with
failure as a bed fellow. Night after night, we re-visited in
our dreams the many lovely places that our searching had
discovered to us. We were like the fisherman who set out
for pike and came home with water lillies. Our days were
not altogether lost.

We came to know Medonte as few can ever know it. We
visited the ruins of early trading posts and Indian encamp-

ments. We kicked arrow heads and tomahawks out of sandy banks. We walked the banks of winding streams, from their rushy mouths to the gurgling springs that were their mothers. We found strange flowers planted generations ago by early settlers, and growing wild now in old pasture fields, cowslips from England, bluebells from Scotland, teazels from Wales, sweet-scented peonies, lovely moss roses, and great clumps of the now rare double narcissus. We found human bones that told of ancient wars, and lovely vistas that whispered only of peace.

At last there came a day when we could hunt no longer. We were beaten, and we knew it. I had work to do I told Lucy, work that would wait no longer while we wasted our days and scuffed our shoes, stumbling through cow pastures in a stupid search for that which, I was at last convinced, existed only in our adled heads. I cursed the silliness that had saddled us with a landless wreck of a house, a leaning, rotten, roofless wreck of a house. I cursed all valleys, creeks, and waterfalls.

Lucy, more amiable in defeat, shrugged. "I'm going sketching," she said. "I'm going down among those cedars by the creek at the bottom of Stone Wall Hill. I'm going where I won't have to listen to you. Pick me up in time for dinner. You'll have cooled off by then . . . "

Dinner-time came, and I hadn't cooled off. I parked the car by the little bridge at the foot of Stone Wall Hill, and walked off the road into the cedars. I waded through a waste of milk-weed and burdocks. I staggered and stumbled through a wilderness of boulders and old stumps. I turned my ankle in a ground-hog's hole, and cursed him and all his tribe.

Lucy was nowhere in sight, and it didn't occur to me at that moment that I was looking for her on the wrong side of the road. I didn't care if I ever found her. I didn't care if she ever found me. I rubbed my ankle and felt sorry for myself. I stared about, seeing the place through a fog of disgruntlement, a miasmic fog of brown fed-upness.

"A bloody desert," I told myself. "Pastured to death ... too thin and cold to grow beans ... would starve a sheep ... bugs by the bagful ... stumps by the ton ... stones galore ... snakes, toads, newts, frogs, slugs, brrr ... !"

And yet the creek was rather pretty, as it wound and turned among the trees at the bottom of the steep little ravine just ahead. Huge old timbers, lying half buried in the burbling water, told of a pioneer dam that had been. A saw mill, or a grist mill, had whirred and clacked there many years ago. The old earthworks, which had helped hold the creek water and form the mill pond, still stood.

Uphill from where I sat, there was a rough bit of pasture, studded with flowering weeds and runty poplar trees. Downhill, a row of solemn cedars edged a narrow valley that ran from the roadway to the side of a flat depression that marked the old pond bottom. A jack-rabbit, crouched in the shadow of a stump, regarded me thoughtfully.

"Starve acres," I told him of the long ears. "No wonder the dam went out! Even creek water wouldn't willingly stay here very long."

It seemed to me that the rabbit's nose twitched in disagreement. It was ridiculous. I grinned. I began to feel better. Slowly, ever so slowly, the fog of disgruntlement lifted from my eyes. There is magic in a grin, or in the twitch of a rabbit's nose. There must be, for it slowly dawned on me as I sat there, that the wilderness I was sitting in, the desert I had been cursing, was actually the very Eden that Lucy and I had been looking for so frantically for so many days. I grinned again. We had travelled miles in our frantic searching, and here, at the bottom of Stone Wall Hill, almost within sight of the old house, was our dream come true. We had passed it a hundred times.

The very creek that Lucy and I had dreamed of, and

had despaired of finding, was winding and laughing in front of me. The chicken range and goat pasture we needed was in the bit of flower-starred hillside in front of me. The bee-yard site we hoped for lay perfectly in the little cedar-edged valley below. The knoll on which I was sitting was just what was needed for the old house. It was high and dry, commanding creek and bee-yard, and looking out over smiling miles of surrounding farmlands.

I had to find Lucy. I raced up and down the little valley, through the cedars on both sides of the road, calling for Lucy, looking for Lucy. She wasn't to be found. I went up the hill to the old house. She wasn't there. I went home and found her seated under the apple tree, sipping a cool drink, and preparing a pointed little speech about people who failed to keep appointments. She had walked home. I told her the news. She finished her drink.

Later that night we sat together in the moonlight on the little knoll in the valley by the creek. We sat and planned our house site, our garden and our chicken house, our bee-yard and our lawn. The stars looking down on us, must have thought us completely mad, as we paced among the rocks and pine stumps, deciding where rose bushes and fruit trees should grow. It did not matter at all to us what the stars thought. It did not matter at all that we did not know who owned the place, and that we had no reason at all for believing that whoever owned it would sell it to us.

Somehow, we knew that the owner would sell. The land was so rough, so broken up, so cut up by ravines and hollows, so filled with stumps and boulders, so run out and thin, so useless to a farmer, that we could not imagine a hard-headed country man refusing a good price for it. While the place to our bemused eyes was a corner of paradise dropped into Medonte by mistake, we retained just enough of our common sense to realize that to a farmer it was mere waste land—starve acres indeed.

As events proved, we were quite right. The owner, at first unable to believe that any sane person would want the place at any price, jumped at the chance to sell, at a price that made us jump. The land became ours, for at least three times its farming worth, and once again the telephone lines of the district hummed, this time with the word that the two city idiots who had bought the old wreck on the hill had now bought four acres of waste land by the creek. It was even said that they planned to move the old house to the creek-side and live in it.

"More money than brains . . . "

"Such simple folk . . . "

Lucy and I studied our bank books. We were in no position to argue this last of the farm folks' judgment of us. *Simple* was the kindest word we called ourselves.

# ₃

## *We Tear the House Down*

WE PUT OUR BANK BOOKS AWAY. WE LET THE GODS, AND our creditors, worry about our finances. We had no time to waste on such trifles. We had our house—an abandoned wreck on a hilltop. We had our land—four acres of hummocky waste-land by a creek. We had now to bring the two together. We went to the town and bought overalls. We bought tools. We sped our overalled legs into the old house on the hilltop and sank the snouts of our new wrecking bars into the rain-stained plaster of the parlour wall.

For a week we worked in a choking fog of lime dust, tearing the inch-thick plaster from ancient hand-split lathes. For a week we heaved and grunted on the ends of our wrecking bars, yanking corroded wrought-iron nails out of petrified studs. We made our own dust bowl there on the hilltop, and had we died in it, as at times we feared we might, future explorers would have found perfect plaster casts of our lungs lying among our bones in the wreckage.

We worked alone, simply because we could not find anybody hardy enough, or foolish enough, to work with us. We worked from dawn until dark, and quit work each night too weary even to snarl at each other. We crawled home to our gritty beds with hair and eyebrows white as snow and stiff as wire, and with our skins so dried by, and permeated with plaster dust that they crackled as we walked. We despaired of ever getting the place cleared of the awful stuff, and pleaded among our friends for help.

We found that, suddenly, we had no friends. We tried among our relatives, and a brother, then a hard rock miner

and now a doctor, volunteered to lend a hand. He worked
with us for half a day and then fled, leaving behind him
no word of his intention to quit, and no clue as to the
haven he sought. Farmer neighbours came to the smoking
windows with red bandanas held to their mouths, and with
a fiendish twinkle in their eyes. We knew what they were
thinking. We offered them work.

*"And they folded their tents like the Arabs,*
  *And silently stole away . . . "*

Lucy and I burrowed like two-legged termites into the
vitals of the old house. We tore at the rotten floor boards,
to find that they were fastened with spikes of hand-wrought
iron to cedar logs three feet thick, and as long as the house
was wide. The big logs had been flattened on their top
sides to hold a level floor, and charred all over to keep out
decay. After over 100 years in sub-floor damp and darkness they were for the most part, still sound and capable
of yet another hundred years of service.

Though we searched diligently for relics of the building's
pioneer past, hoping to find a tarnished coin carrying the
fat head of George IV, a rusted bullet mould, or a little
brown whiskey jug, we found nothing so exciting. We did
find the old front door key lying just where it had slipped
and fallen, unguessed generations ago, and we picked it
up, half expecting to hear a ghostly voice exclaim over
our shoulders,

"Well, drat it all! So that's where the plaguey thing
went!"

We came at last to the door frames, and the window
frames, ponderous slabs of virgin pine held in place by a
multitude of hardwood pegs. The pegs, two feet long,
were driven firmly into the hearts of the hewn timbers of
the walls, and time had sealed them there. Trying to draw
them was like trying to draw the plug out of the throat
of an extinct volcano. Lucy and I tried. We heaved, and

hung, and swung together on the end of our crowbar, like
two ripe plums on a tree. We grunted and groaned, and
the pegs creaked derision. We could have blasted those
window frames free. We could have taken an axe and
chopped them free. We did neither. We hunted a carpenter.

We found the one man in the entire district who had
the sympathy and skill to give the old house the job we
wanted, the job the old house deserved. A country carpenter with pride in his craft, and an inborn kindliness
which found its way into his hands whenever they touched
old things, took over the job we had so clumsily begun.
The old house seemed to sigh, and relax in his hands. The
great pine timbers gave up their hardwood pegs almost
eagerly to him, for he drew them easily, with a tiny wrecking bar. The heavy old rafters surrendered their rotten
roof boards. The second storey floor joists came down without a murmur of protest. The old house simply melted
quietly away as our carpenter moved over it, and seven
neatly numbered piles of lumber grew by the roadside.
Soon all that was left of it were four gaunt walls, a fortress-
like oblong of gray hand-hewn timbers.

Generations ago, moccasined settlers had travelled many
miles over dim bush trails to help in the raising of those
mighty walls. Bearded faces and buckskin shirts had pressed
the then bright-sided timbers, steadying them as they were
heaved and hauled by shouting men and lowing oxen up
the long skid poles to their appointed beds. The raising
had been a grand success. A half a hundred bearded lips,
wet with whiskey and strong spruce beer, had said so. The
wild wail of a home-made fiddle had insisted upon it.
Cavorting women and squealing children had agreed.

Now, in the quiet of a summer afternoon, the big timbers,
bright-sided no longer, but fingered by the years to a silvery
gray, were coming down. A chapter in their lives had been

written. Their hilltop song was sung. Once again the long
skid poles were leaned against them. Once again the men
of the district, clean-shaven now, and dressed in faded
overalls, gathered for the event. They came, not on foot,
or behind yoked oxen, but by truck and by car, and on
wagons that plunged and rattled behind plodding pairs of
slow, big-muscled horses. They came, like their ancestors
before them, to help and to wonder at the artistry of the
axework, to stare in frank open-mouthed amazement at the
smooth perfection of the ancient hewing.

The old house, the old lady of the hilltop, was about to
go on a journey. The big timbers, all carefully numbered,
were tilted out of their mortered beds, slid on to the skid
poles, and lowered by logging chains to the yawning bol-
sters of the rumbling wagons that drew up, each in its
turn, on to the grass below them. One after another the
big sticks went down. One after another the wagons were
loaded. The horses leaned in their traces, and drew their
gray burdens out of the shadow of the shrinking walls,
out through the drunken road gate, down the long hillside
to the new house site being made ready among the stones
and cedars by Moonstone Creek.

The stars that night found an empty space on the hilltop, an empty space in a ruined garden, wreckage, and a
lonely wooden pump.

# PART 2

## Sawdust and Daisies

*"Mine be a cot beside the hill;*
*A bee-hive's hum shall soothe my ear;*
*A willowy brook that turns a mill*
*With many a fall shall linger near . . .*

*Around my ivied porch shall spring*
*Each fragrant flower that drinks the dew,*
*And Lucy, at her wheel, shall sing*
*In russet-gown and apron blue . . . "*

S. ROGERS, 1763

# 4

## *We Rummage the Past*

To BUILD A HOUSE IN THE COUNTRY, WHERE HAMMERS rise and fall in time to bird-song, where the skree of the saw is heard as an overtone to the murmur of creek water, where even the hearty cursing of the workmen seems but a continuation of a chipmunk's chattered rage, is a joy not given to everyone. Lucy and I cavorted like goatlings among the lumber piles by the creek. We set up a fire-place of field stones at the edge of the cedars, and there, day after day, among ripening blackberries and bearded golden-rod. we had our lunches and our dinners. We spent long evenings, chin deep in daisies, planning the last detail of our home-to-be.

We knew what we wanted. The old place had suffered many changes. Generations of improvers had had their

way with it, tearing out the heavy beams of the old low
ceiling, and putting in sawn planks at a higher level. They
had torn the old beaded pine boards from the walls, and put
up lath and plaster. They had replaced many of the old
small-paned windows with characterless large-paned sash.
They had even torn out the old fireplace and put in its
stead a spindly chimney and an iron cook stove.

We wanted the old beams, or beams exactly like them,
back in the niches that the pioneer builders had cut for
them in the old walls. We wanted beaded boards back
on the walls. We wanted board and batten doors, wrought-
iron hardware, a circular wooden staircase, a big open
fireplace, a plain mantel shelf, and squat fat chimneys of
hand-made brick. We wanted everything to be as it had
been in the beginning, and we were to learn that we wanted
a lot.

While our workmen busied themselves at the house-site
digging a cellar hole, and building foundations, we scoured
the countryside, hunting in the ruins of other old pioneer
homes for bits and pieces that might be useful in the
restoration of ours. We found mouldering in a straw barn
on a neighbouring farm, three heavy hand-hewn beams
that would fit our ceiling. We found three more, half-buried
in manure, in a near-by barnyard. We drove excitedly
across the township when rumour came, on the tail of a
high wind, to tell us that an old log barn had collapsed
during the gale, and that fine hewn timbers, up to eighty
feet long, could be had for the proverbial song. Higgledy-
piggledy, we added to the stock pile of odds and ends
needed to replace the bits and pieces that generations of
vandals had torn out of our house.

We were, for the most part, lucky in our hunting, and
yet we had our moments of disappointment. There was
the log house that we came upon in the moonlight, and
explored by lantern light. It had been a wilderness man-

sion in its day, by far the finest timber building in the district. It was a pig-pen when we found it. A sow and her litter of eleven small grunters sprawled in a snoring heap in the dung-littered corner of a perfectly proportioned room that was walled, half-way to its beamed ceiling, with honey-brown panelling of clear, virgin pine. The narrowest board was nearly four feet wide, and as smooth as satin.

"I'd like to buy those boards," I told the owner.

"Nope," he answered. "The chinking is gone from between the logs back of 'em. They keep the draft off the pigs."

"I'll buy the boards at your own price, and send carpenters with lumber to put in a lining that will keep your pigs warm forever."

"Nope." The reply was an adamant grunt.

"Do you mind if we look upstairs?" asked Lucy.

"Nope."

We went up a bannistered staircase, that had once been beautiful, into a large bedroom. It was filled with chickens. An old spool bed was doing duty as a roost.

"I'll buy that bed," I told the owner, who had followed us up.

"Nope."

"You don't want it." I protested.

"The chickens do."

"I'll buy the bed and put in a roost for you and your chickens."

"Nope."

We went downstairs again, for a comforting glance at the look of intelligence in the old sow's eyes. We went into another once-lovely room and found, still hanging in the great stone fireplace that was there, a magnificent example of the pioneer blacksmith's art, a perfectly proportioned wrought-iron crane.

"What are you going to do with that?" I asked the owner.

"It'll come in handy for something."

"What, for instance?"

"It'll cut up into drift pins—good drift pins, too."

I didn't ask him to sell. The thought of another stupid "Nope" jerking out of that loose-lipped, tobacco-stained mouth was too much. We left him with his panelled pig-pen, his carved walnut chicken roosts, and his wrought-iron drift-pins-to-be. We left with the silent hope that some-day, somehow, he would trip on that lovely ruined stair-case and break his unwashed neck.

We went another day at twilight, through a flock of resting sheep, into another old timber house, a tiny place this time, a wee cabin in a valley by a stream. We walked through a doorway that had not been closed for a genera-tion, into a room so warm in feeling, so redolent still of loving hearts and hands that, despite its emptiness and the filth that littered it, neither Lucy nor I would have been surprised to hear old voices bid us welcome.

The usual beaded boards of tawny pine covered the walls. The ceiling was whitewashed between time-blackened beams. The doors were let into the partitions at either end of the room we stood in. Two led into tiny bedrooms. A third led into a roomy closet. The fourth opened on to a twisty staircase that led up, beside a great stone chimney, into a cosy slant-ceilinged room above. An old pine settle still stood before the hearth, and in one of the bedrooms there was still a big four-poster bed.

It was the old mantel-piece that caught and held Lucy's eye, and mine. It was fine, of early colonial design, as unmarked and unblemished as it was the day its proud maker had set it there over 100 years ago. Somehow it gave the friendly old room a beauty and a dignity that generations of dirt and neglect could not touch.

Lucy and I wanted that mantel. The days of the old house were numbered. That much was obvious to the most casual observer. The sill logs were rotted into nothingness. The plate logs were mere streaks of rotten punk. The rafters were buckled. The whole place was leaning, wracked and broken, beyond hope of salvage or repair. It seemed a pity that this sweet masterpiece of pioneer craftmanship and design, this old pine mantel, should be lost in the general ruin. After a bit of a search we found the owner. He would not sell.

"It's the old family homestead," he explained. "I'm keeping it for sentimental reasons."

We looked at each other hopelessly. It was hard to reconcile his sentiments with the holes in the roof, the open doors and glassless windows, with the rot, the dirt, and decay. A year later the old place collapsed, and the tawny pine boards and the lovely mantel were cut up for firewood.

# 5

## *We Hire a Witch*

A WIRY LITTLE MAN WITH BULL-LIKE SHOULDERS AND A swarthy face, wandered in off the concession line one afternoon, and stood silently watching the work in progress at our house site. He spoke to no one, and no one spoke to him. An hour passed. The sun slanted westwards. The workmen prepared to go home. The little man still stood by the cellar hole, swaying a little on his short legs, spitting tobacco juice meditatively at a near-by mortar box.

"Well," I asked him finally, "what can I do for you?"

"Nothin'," he told me. "I kinda figgered I could do something for you."

"Yes?"

"Yeah, I'm a witcher."

"A what?"

"A water witcher," he explained. "I witch fer water— I find water. I dig wells. Figgered you might want a good well on this place."

I wasn't impressed. Water divining was so much mumbo-jumbo to me. Still, we did want a well on the place, a good well that would fill with cold spring water and stay filled, regardless of how we used it. And I was curious to see how this water-witch would go about his business of water witching. I had never seen a water diviner at work.

"Go ahead," I told him.

The little man with the big shoulders went to his car and brought out a forked twig. "Hazel wood," he explained, with a shy smile. "Some call it witch hazel wood." He went out on to the hillside, and with two ends of the fork held firmly in his two hands, and with the butt end of the twig pointing directly ahead of him, began pacing slowly back and forth across the field. I followed him, sceptical, but fascinated.

"What happens?" I asked.

"You'll see."

Back and forth across the field we went, back and forth, back and forth, while the sunset filled the western sky with fire, and the shadows lengthened over the darkening hills. Suddenly the water-witch stopped his pacing. The knuckles of his hands whitened with strain. The forked twig in his hands twisted like a snake. He seemed to be struggling. The forks splintered. The thick butt of the hazel wood branch shuddered downwards, as though something powerful and invisible was pulling it down.

"There is your spring," said the water diviner. "It's running strong, about six feet down."

I didn't believe him, and so he walked the field again, this time with an iron crowbar balanced across two fingers of his left hand. When he came to the spot where the twig had twisted, the thick end of the crowbar dipped suddenly. I leaned forward and grasped the bar just ahead of his hand. I felt the strong down pull.

"The spring is still there," he declared, with a sardonic grin. "An' it's still jest six feet down."

I still didn't believe him, and so the water diviner walked the fields yet a third time, this time with his heavy old-fashioned watch held motionless at the end of his watch chain, at arm's length, and breast high from the ground. When his pacing brought him again to the spot where the iron bar had dipped, where the twig had twisted, the watch began spinning on the end of its chain, at first slowly, and then rapidly, so rapidly that I thought that it would twist the soft gold links apart. I looked at his hand. It was rock steady. There was no sign there that he was helping his

time-piece spin. Still I was unconvinced. I shook my head.
It was all so impossible. It was still hocus-pocus to me.

"Look, Mister," stormed the diviner, his dark face glowing with rage, "for two dollars a foot I'll dig yer well fer
you. If I don't find more water than you an' yer whole
damned family can ever use, I'll pay you two dollars a foot
fer diggin' on yer blasted hill!"

I accepted his offer.

Never was a man less like a man, and more like a woodchuck, or mole, than that little water diviner. He did not
dig his way into the earth of our hillside. He burrowed
into it, grasping his short handled shovel but a few inches
above the blade, and using it exactly as a digging woodchuck
might use its paws. Dirt spattered out of the deepening
well-hole in a steady shower that first littered, and then
buried the grass and flowers around the well site. Down
and down he went, knee deep, waist deep, shoulder deep.
Soon only his bobbing head, then only the tip of his flailing
shovel, and finally only a constant shower of flying earth
remained to tell the passer-by of the frantic activity that
was going on in the bottom of the hole on the hillside.

At a depth of six feet, where sand met clay, he struck
water, just as he had said he would. The water came in,
first as a thin trickle, and then as it cleared a way for itself,
in an increasing stream. The water-witch called me to
the side of the well-hole, and pointed at the rising flood.
He said nothing. He just pointed, but out of the two slits
in the ball of clay that was his head, his dark eyes glared
triumphantly.

We had our water, but in order to hold it, we had to
make a reservoir for it, to dig on down through the blue
clay another twenty, or thirty feet. The water diviner
built himself a box-like arrangement of boards and scantlings, a few inches smaller than the well-hole. As he dug,
he pulled this cage down after him, and built on to the

top, so that he had always, from top to bottom of the well-shaft, a wooden shell to protect him from cave-ins that might otherwise have buried him alive. When he had dug to a point where he could no longer throw the clay clear of the well mouth, he rigged a gallows over it, and hooked on a pulley and a rope, and a heavy iron bucket.

It was our well-digger's misfortune that the helper I found for him was a neighbourhood farmer with a perverted sense of humour. It was this man's job to draw, at first by hand, and later with the help of a grey horse, the mud and water filled bucket out of the well, empty it, and return it to the digger below. All went well until he noticed that a knot in the bucket rope came to his hand just before the lowered bucket reached the head of the well-digger. From that time on there was no peace on the hillside above Moonstone Creek. There were bangs, and clangs, and yells, and curses, and shrieks of idiotic laughter.

The well-digger's helper had a new way of returning a mud bucket to a well-digger. He simply tossed it into the well-mouth, to fall with a clattering bang down the long wooden shaft, to stop when the knot reached his hand, with a sudden, shuddering jerk, within inches of the cowering digger's shaking head. In vain did the well-digger protest. This was his helper's way of returning the bucket to him, and return it this way he would, or not at all. Rather than be held up in his work by lack of a helper, for I could get him no other, he put up with this nonsense, but it was a shaken, and shaking man that came out of the well-hole each night.

"Gad, man!" his helper would exclaim, as the shaking, cursing, bundle of clay that was a man rose out of the well-mouth at quitting time, "It's all in the way of a joke, and meant for no harm. Gad, man, and I wouldn't hurt a hair of your head, if you have hair at all under that filthy ball of clay that might or might not be a hat. Gad, man . . . "

The shaking of the well-digger would increase. He would chatter with impotent rage, wave his hands in the air, and then totter away to his car; yet somehow he managed to summon up enough nerve, or stubborness, to continue. Day after day he returned to the job, digging himself deeper and deeper into the earth. Day after day, a hundred times a day, he winced from the heavy iron bucket that clanged down upon him from the well-mouth, never knowing when the oaf above might miss the knot and kill him with his fun. He dug until a second spring broke in on him, and he could no longer control the flood.

We had our well.

# 6

## *We Put the House Up Again*

THE FIELDS WERE TAWNY WITH AUTUMN, AND APPLES
were red on the bough, before the silver-gray walls of the
old timber house that had once crowned Stone Wall Hill
began to rise again. Rain had plagued us, slowing up the
work on some days, stopping it altogether on others. Dripping workmen had thrown down their rusty tools in disgust,
and left for indoors work in town. It was the wettest autumn
in years, old-timers said.

At last the work of make-ready was finished. At last the
sun rose clear. Once again the heavy farm horses of the
neighbourhood snorted and leaned in their traces. Once
again the burly skid poles splintered and groaned. Once
again the smooth gray sticks of hand-hewn pine climbed
skyward, to find rest again, with scrunch of relief, in the
niches from which we had twisted them when we tore the
old house down.

Lucy and I, barred by our lack of experience from helping
in the work, stood uselessly by. We bit our lips, and held
our breaths, and kept our restless fingers in our pockets.
We were scared. Dreams, work, and plans, all hung in the
balance as the big, chain-bound timbers mounted the shuddering skids. Did a leaf blow in the face of one of the strain-
ing horses, did a stinging fly light on its flank, did a startled
beast plunge forward, dragging its load beyond the wall-
line into the cellar-hole beyond, did a skid-pole break, or
a chain-link snap, all that we had done would be undone
in an instant.

The workmen grinned at our obvious anxiety, and yet

they, too, were tense. The piling of those heavy walls was
a testing of their skill. It was a testing, too, of the rusty
barnyard equipment that was all they had to work with.
There could be no mistakes, no mishaps. The big timbers,
despite their burliness, were brittle with age. A fall of even
a yard might shiver them. A bump might crack them. And
there was no timber yard this side of Jordan where a
damaged one could be replaced.

"Use yer best words on 'em," warned a helper, "but treat
'em like you would a pretty gal."

Luck was with us still. No wind-blown leaf, no hungry
fly, marred the smooth perfection of the raising. No skid-
pole broke. No chain-link snapped. The big pine timbers
crunched sweetly, one after another, into their accustomed
beds. The old mortised corners knitted neatly together again,
so neatly indeed, that between lifts the wondering workmen
gathered around them, attempting vainly to thrust the thin
points of their jack-knife blades into the ancient, axe-cut
corner-joints. The plate log went on. The skid poles came
down. The sweating horses were led off to rest under the
spreading boughs of the fat birch by the creek. Lucy and I,
exhausted by the tension of the day, rested with them.

As the days sped by, the house grew before our delighted
eyes. The ceiling beams that we had salvaged from the
wrecked barns and barnyards were cut to length, and spiked
and pegged into place. The rafters and roof boards went
on. The window and door frames went in. Long cedar
wedges were cut to size, and sledge-hammered into the
yawning gaps between the old timbers of the wall. A mortar
made of lime, sand, and hair, was worked in over them,
both from the inside and the outside of the house. So the
wall was chinked, made tight, and wind and waterproof.

Day after day, long hours after the last of our carpenters
had laid down their tools and gone home for the night, Lucy
and I pottered about the house-site, laying out lumber for

the morrow, broaching new kegs of nails, setting out new pots of tar and creosote, new bags of lime. We worked by twilight, by moonlight, and by lantern light, making all ready for the next day's work. We had to economize where we could. We had hired good workmen, at good wages, for their skill, and we did not want them wasting their time, and our money, wandering about in search of needed materials. There was, we had found long since, no cheaper unskilled labour than our own.

Remembering the old timber and log houses that we had visited and explored, we planned the interior of our house in a manner traditional among pioneer builders in the district. We had no reason to suppose that our house, in the beginning, had been any different. Our front door opened directly on to a large living room that took up the entire central portion of the house. Two doors were let into each of the end partitions of this big room. The east end doors opened on to a kitchen and a bedroom, that was to become a photographic dark room. The west end doors, flanking a big fireplace of hand-made brick, led on one side of the fireplace into a roomy closet, and on the other side on to a flight of cellar steps. We lined the walls with beaded pine. We set a heavy pine timber on end in one corner of the living room, and built a circular wooden staircase around it. Upstairs we made another large room, my writing room, and two smaller rooms, another bedroom and a tiny crowded bit of a room that has proved to be, in the eyes of our neighbours, the crowning glory of all our enterprise. We fitted storage closets into every possible corner, and lined the walls with bookshelves.

So far we kept our house faithful to its pioneer past. It was only when we came to such things as lighting, sanitation, and water, that we left the old days unregretfully behind. Lucy and I had lived long enough with oil lamps to loathe the smelly things. We put electricity in. We had bathed often enough in galvanized wash tubs to have corrugated hips. We put in a porcelain bathtub, a wash basin, and a couple of sinks.

We like to think that our old house blushed thankfully, and with modest pride, when we, after many conferences involving bank books and plumbers' estimates, installed a glowing example of that most precious of all inventions, a water closet that actually flushed. It was, like our house, the first in history on our concession line.

"New-fangled nonsense," snorted a grey-haired farmer of the next hill, blissfully ignorant that the water closet, like Shakespeare's plays, is a product of Elizabethan genius.

"Fussy, ain't they?" agreed his wife, and came visiting, primarily to see the gadget work.

The days grew colder. The windows were glazed and put in place. Night frosts killed the asters. The outside doors were hung. The creek froze. The chimneys were finished. A sudden snow storm blocked the concession line, burying the fences and stripping the last dead leaves from the hardwood trees. Some of the workmen parked their cars on the ploughed side road a mile distant, and walked to the job on skis. Others decided that they had worked long enough on the old house by Moonstone Creek, and stayed home. The inside doors, made like the walls of beaded boards, were fitted. Hardwood floors were laid, upstairs of beach wood, downstairs of red birch. To the pungency of fresh sawdust and new lumber, was added the cloying sweetness of linseed oil, and the reek of turpentine.

With the arrival of our pine mantel shelf, a poor shadow of that thing of beauty which a sentimentalist had cut up for firewood, but still the crowning glory of our fireplace, the task of restoring to use and loveliness the old gray wreck that we had found on Stone Wall Hill was completed. Lucy and I carried the big shelf a long mile from the ploughed side-road, down the drifted concession line to Moonstone creek. A cold wind raved in our faces, choking and blinding us with driven snow that stung like whip-lash. We wallowed, and we cursed. We wrestled like terriers with our mantel shelf, which the devil-fingered wind tried to tear from our grasp, and which, when we would not let go, rolled us and shelf together headlong into drift and ditch. We got to the house-site at sunset, just at quitting time, and our carpenter, to please us, stayed late and put it in place by lantern light.

Our house was done.

# PART 3

## Wood Smoke and Snow

*When icicles hang by the wall,*
*And Dick the shepherd blows his nail,*
*And Tom bears logs into the hall,*
*And milk comes frozen home in pail,*
*When blood be nipp'd and ways be foul,*
*Then nightly sings the staring owl,*
*        To who . . .*

SHAKESPEARE, 1617

# 7

*We Move In*

THE DAY THAT LUCY AND I BROUGHT THE FIRST LOAD OF OUR
household goods to the old house by the creek was a golden
day, filled with that faint tinkle of tiny bells that is made by
melting snow. Slowly shrinking drifts still reached shining
white tongues across the concession line, closing it to wheeled
traffic. Day-old fox tracks, melted by the sun to a colossal
size, ran in the snow beside the top rails of buried fences.
We rode on a lurching wood sleigh, behind steaming horses,
out to the ploughed main road where the red truck that had
brought our possessions from town waited for us.

It was a glorious ride, with winter underfoot and summer
overhead. We lay back in the sweet-smelling hay that
covered the big racks with which the sleighs had been fitted
for the occasion, and blinked at the sun. The horses snorted.

37

The sleigh runners whispered. A following collie barked
excitedly. The sky was a blue meadow in which clouds like
lambs grazed slowly. This was what we had dreamed after.
This was what we had worked for, the peace and quiet of a
lonely concession line, the nearness of things eternal, and
time to savour them.

We were not long transferring our possessions from the
truck to the hay-racks. They were not many, and the truck
driver, muttering about "gawd-fersaken wildernesses", was
impatient to get away. There was the heavy oak dresser
that we had bought in a city second-hand shop, and the old
spool bed that we had found in a junk shop in a neighbouring
town. There was the quaint walnut kitchen table that Lucy's
mother had fished out of her attic for us, and there were
other bits and pieces that my mother had found for us in her
cluttered storage rooms. There were Lucy's tools, my books,
camera, and typewriters. There were dishes, and pictures,
and a length of garden hose. There was little enough to
furnish a house, but more than enough to make a home.

Home! That was it. When we had finished our loading,
and turned the horses' heads away from the highway, away
from town, back down the concession line, we would actually
be going home. Our years of town and city living would be,
at long last, at an end. Our bridges were burned. We had
given up the key to the little drab house in town. In an
hour's time we would be back by Moonstone Creek, lighting
our own fire, on our own hearth, under our own roof tree.
Home, indeed!

"Men," said Thoreau, "leave the desperate city for the
desperate country, and there console themselves with the
bravery of mink and muskrats." Well, we could do that too.
We had had enough of the smug meanness of small towns,
enough of the cold self-seeking of big cities. We had found
neither comfort, nor happiness in them, and little to respect.
If worst came to the worst, if our dreams turned out to be

pipe-dreams after all, we would at least, as Thoreau pointed out, be able to console ourselves with the bravery of muskrats, a something not sold with their skins in city fur shops, but common in our creek.

Lucy and I watched the red truck that had brought our belongings from town grow small in the distance. The truck driver had felt sorry for us, buried alive in a bloody backwoods, as he put it. We had felt sorry for him, but had not said so. Our hearts were too full for argument. Our minds were too busy with memories. Lucy's eyes were misty. My mind reached out from the trampled snow of the concession line, where we stood alone, holding hands like two lost school children, to the fateful night when, while riding home from work in a crowded street car, I read these words by King Henry VI, in a pocket edition of Shakespeare's Plays:

> "Oh God! methinks it were a happy life,
> To be no better than a homely swain—
> To sit upon a hill as I do now,
> To carve out dials quaintly, point by point,
> Thereby to see the minutes how they run,
> How many make the hour full complete;
> How many hours bring about the day;
> How many days will finish up the year;
> How many years a mortal man may live.
> When this is known, then to divide the times;
> So many hours must I tend my flock;
> So many hours must I take my rest;
> So many hours must I contemplate;
> So many hours must I sport myself;
> So many days my ewes have been with young;
> So many weeks ere the poor fools will ean;
> So many months ere I shall shear the fleece;
> So many minutes, hours, days, months, years
> Passed over to the end they were created,
> Would bring white hairs until a quiet grave.

Ah, what a life were this! how sweet! how lovely!
Gives not the hawthorn bush a sweeter shade
To shepherds looking on their silly sheep
Than doth a rich embroidered canopy."

The street-car rattled and clanged. I closed my book
and put it back into my pocket. It is not every man who
has a momentous decision made for him, by a poet centuries dead. A king had dreamed, as I had dreamed, or
was it Will, dreaming back to his lost youth in Stratford?
Well, I was no king to be fobbed off with a crown, or a
playwright to sell for fame his birthright of green fields.
My income gave me no reason to hope of ever owning an
embroidered canopy. With careful planning we might just
manage a hawthorne bush.

The future seemed rosy to Lucy and me as we drove back
down the drifted concession line, swaying with the wood
sleigh, and perched like crows atop our piled-up goods.
We had bought our hawthorne tree, and put an old timber
house beside it. Come spring we would add a studio, also
of hewn pine. We would build a honey-house, and a
poultry house, and a goat pen. We would fill our yard with
white-hived colonies of honey-bees. We would fill our hillside field with chickens, ducks, and geese. We would plant
a garden and an orchard.

I, who had written of scull-duggery and meanness and
crowded streets, would write now of a clean countryside,
of bees, and goats, and self-respecting pigs. I would turn
my camera from wrecked automobiles, and wrecked human-
ity, to green fields, rail fences, and tall hills. Lucy, the
artist, the sculptor, the wood engraver, would take her
art out of the stuffiness of a city studio into the freshness of
the farm house and the farmyard. We would put a sign
by our gate reading:

HONEY AND FRESH EGGS FOR SALE

ALSO

SCULPTURE AND PHOTOGRAPHS

POEMS AND WOODCUTS

AND

SPRING CHICKEN

For the gate we planned another sign, bearing the name of our home, "The Owl Pen."

# 8

## *We Clean Stove Pipes*

LUCY AND I EXPECTED TO BE BORED. SNOW WAS ON THE ground, and the ground was frozen. Even seed catalogues pall after a time. Outside work, with the chaotic mess that our building activities had made of our once pretty valley, was out of the question. We had no cattle to tend, no pigs to feed, no chickens to fuss with. We were, we felt, marking time until spring, and we wondered what on earth we would do with ourselves once the furniture was set in place, and the curtains hung. Spring seemed years away.

The days passed, and the weeks passed, and we were not bored. A multitude of tiny, time-devouring tasks came constantly to hand. Full weeks grew into full months. We were as busy in our new-old house as a pair of wood-chucks might be in a new burrow. Though we got up early, and went to bed late, our days were too short for the work that pressed on us.

There was, for instance, the matter of fuel. A monstrous mountain of tree trunks filled our work yard. Every piece of it had to be split, and split again, into billets that would fit our wood stove. I got me a splitting axe. For the rest of the winter, rain, blow, snow, hail, or shine, I spent at least an hour every day in that work yard, flailing like a demented banshee at that cordwood, learning the hard way the subtle country art of wood-chopping.

According to Lucy, only two sizes of wood came to her wood-box that first winter we spent in the country. It came too big, and it came too small. Too big, apparently, burned too slowly to give her the heat her cooking required. Too small burned too quickly, burned her bread to a crisp, and went out. She demanded a medium sort of stick, a compromise as it were, the sort of stick that burns steadily and hotly, cooking her cakes to a turn, and leaving behind a bed of glowing coals to keep them warm. I just couldn't split that kind of stick.

Wood is a magnificent sort of fuel. From the time it topples as a great tree in the forest, to the time it is carried out of a house as a small bucket of ashes, to be used in sweetening garden soil, or the dropping boards in a chicken house, it rewards the user. A mixture of different kinds of hardwood sticks in a kitchen wood-box is like nothing else on earth so much as an anthology of fine poetry. There is a kind for every mood.

Alive or dead, in the cutting or in the burning, trees keep their personality. Maple splits deliberately, burns with a quiet dignity, and leaves behind a splendid bed of coals. Beech splits easily, and burns gently to a fine ash. Birch, forever dramatic, flakes unpredictably under the splitting axe, burns urgently, as though impatient of its last task on earth, as though eager to be gone. Elm, that poor despised pariah of the woodlands, has been known to rouse a patient wood chopper to language that could be heard a mile from the wood yard, yet it burns with a solemn slowness, providing a perfect log for an overnight fire, and leaving behind it, as a fitting shroud for its few dim coals, a mighty mound of ash.

It is a poor countryman who cannot walk into a farm house and tell, the instant he crosses the threshold, the kind of wood that is burning in the kitchen stove. It is not smoke that he smells, but a subtle pervading perfume. The scent of burning maple, for instance, is as different from the scent of burning beech as is the fragrance of roses from that of violets. The sweet spice smell of smouldering birch is something that might have come out of a red god's treasure chest. There is also another smell that comes on occasion to a farm house where wood is burned, the acrid reek of creosote, a reek straight out of hell.

When that smell came to the Owl Pen, Lucy and I knew what to do, at least we thought we did. The stove-pipes needed cleaning. Lucy spread old newspapers in strategic places. I brought in a step-ladder and a pair of pliers. We were a happy, loving couple as I mounted the ladder, and undid the wires that held the stove-pipes parallel with the kitchen ceiling.

"Be careful, darling," said Lucy.

"I will, my pet," said I.

The next moment Lucy disappeared from sight in a cloud of soot. The stove-pipe, bereft of its wire support, had suddenly buckled out of an elbow, and come apart in my hands.

"Accidents will happen," I observed philosophically.

"You clumsy ox," choked Lucy, stumbling blindly out of the black fog that enveloped her, and barging into the step-ladder.

"Careful!" I screamed. Too late. The ladder swayed drunkenly. I jumped for the stove top. The long length of pipe that I was supporting broke again. One end of it came down with a clump on Lucy's already spattered head. The other end of it clattered down into the handle of the warming oven. The oven door came down on the end of a spoon that was sticking out of a jar of fat. The jar upset. Fat, jar, spoon, soot and stove-pipe, cascaded down over the polished stove top, and me.

"Of all the useless . . . " I began, and stopped suddenly, warned perhaps by a savage gleam in the soot-ringed eyes of my loving wife.

"Say it," she dared me. "Go on, say it, you . . . you . . .

you . . . " She pointed a shaking, grubby finger at me. "Ga . . . "

I stepped backwards on the greasy stove top, away from her threatening digit. I skidded, and sat down on the stove pipe, flattening it completely.

"Now look what you made me do!" I stormed.

"I made you do!"

"You made me do!"

"You . . . !"

"You . . . !"

"Listen, darling," said I, with what I hoped was a note of dangerous calmness in my voice, "you are tired. You have been working too hard. You need a change, a holiday. Go and visit your mother for awhile. Go to China. Stay three months. Stay six months. Stay a year." Somehow my voice rose from basso profundo to shrill falsetto. "Perhaps by the time you get back I'll have these blankety-blank stove-pipes up again, this horrible blankety-blank mess that you—yes, you—made me make, cleaned up again. Perhaps . . . "

Lucy's two ordinarily blue eyes glowed like red coals of fire in the blackness of her soot-covered face. She said nothing. She picked the pliers out of a pool of soot and fat on the kitchen floor, and handed them to me. She turned on her heel, slipped, slithered, and marched with extreme dignity, out of the room.

"Why, oh why!" I heard her exclaim as she passed the cat, purring outrageously on the sofa in the living room. "Why did I marry that man?"

The rest is silence.

# 9

## *We Learn About Winter*

AS THE WHITE WEEKS OF WINTER RACED TOWARDS SPRING, and we came to know more of our neighbours than their names and the marks of their boots on the concession line, we learned how they spent the long, cold days of what a silly city poet has somewhere called the "Morte saison", the dead time of the year. Somehow we had always thought of the winter as being a farmer's resting time, a period in which he did no more than chores, sit by the fire, make love to his wife, and read magazines. How wrong we were!

In the winter time, in Medonte, a farmer gets up, not as he does in the summer time when dawn begins to light his bedroom, but many hours before day-break. He dresses with numbed hands, in clothes that are stiff with frost, and stumbles down a dark stairway into the kitchen. The kettle on the back of the kitchen stove, which burns out every night, is frozen solid. Three eggs on the kitchen table are frozen and cracked. He lights a fire in the stove, fills and lights his lantern, and crunches out through deep snow to the well.

Naturally the pump is frozen. With twenty head of cattle, a dozen pigs, a team of horses, and half a hundred hens to water, it would be. He goes on to the barn, routes out the cattle and the horses, and drives them towards the near-by creek. As he passes the drive shed, he puts down his lantern and picks up his axe, with which to cut a drinking-hole in the ice for the thirsty beasts. The first red finger of dawn is crooked in the eastern sky.

Down at the creek the cattle bawl impatiently. The

horses whinney and stamp. The farmer kicks aside the deep snow and cuts a hole in the ice. Dark water burbles out, spreading a dark stain into the snow. The cattle rush it. A wild burst of profanity fills the creek-bottom, as the farmer is pushed knee-deep into the hole he has cut. The cattle regard him with a sort of mild surprise. He comes out shouting his opinion of their ancestors, and wet to the skin.

While their sputtering owner lies on his back on the creek-bank with his feet in the air, emptying the ice-water out of his rubber boots, the unperturbed cattle drink their fill, then one after another, amble slowly back up the hillside to the barn. The farmer stamps after them, sees them all into their stalls, and ties them there. This done, he picks up a battered pair of buckets, and goes back to the creek again, this time for water for the still-penned pigs and fowl. After several splashful trips back and forth up the steep creek-bank, down with the buckets banging his shins, up with spilled ice-water running over his stiffening overalls, he decides that they have had enough water. He knows that he has.

Next in the morning routine on a Medonte farm is the feeding and the cleaning. Up into the cavernous darkness of the mow he goes, to throw down great forkfuls of hay and straw. Down the slippery ladder he crawls again, to shake the new hay into the mangers, to clear the manure and old bedding out of the stalls and put fresh straw in. Then he distributes oats to the horses, chop to the cows, meal to the pigs, and grain to the hens. That finishes it, except for the milking, and his wife joins him in that.

Carrying full pails of steaming, froth-topped milk, the pair of them stumble back through the snow to the farm house. His wife goes on in with the milk. He stops by the woodshed long enough to split the day's supply of wood. This done, he sighs deeply, lights his pipe, and looks up at the sunrise. A jingle, written, though he does not know it, by English Thomas Tusser over 500 years ago, comes to his mind:

> *"Red sky at morning,*
> *A shepherd's warning . . . "*

As it is now late, all of six-thirty, the farmer does not dawdle over his tea and porridge, nor even over his eggs and fried pork. He finishes his breakfast with an extra helping of fried potatoes and a big wedge of apple pie, and grabs his hat. There is a day's work to be done yet, he tells his wife, and that good woman thinking of the milk yet to be separated, the separator yet to be cleaned, of the butter yet to be made, of the washing yet to be done, and of the chicken house that should be tidied, grimly agrees.

As the road is drifted, he will not be able to use his old car. As his bay horse is a bit off colour, he will not be able to use his cutter. The mare is in foal. After all, it is only a few miles across country to the woodlot where he has been earning spring seeding money by cutting cordwood. He puts on a pair of home-made skis and is off. Despite his hurry, he does not forget his shotgun, and on the way manages to knock over a jack rabbit. A destructive pest, he tells himself, but good in the pot. He trudges on, thinking of his two sons at work in distant city factories. If only one of them were home to help . . . Back home, he knows, his wife is thinking of three daughters, also away in city jobs. If only one of them . . . The old farm has been in the family over a hundred years. Now . . . He shrugs.

It is all of eight-thirty before he gets his axe into the butt of the first tree of the day, so he takes no time off for smoking or chatting. He hews silently until noon. Lunch is a sandwich, another piece of apple pie, and a slice of cake. He munches it, huddled in his coat and cap, and seated on the trunk of the last tree down, or, on a stormy day, in a dark over-heated shack knocked up for the occasion. The afternoon is the morning repeated. He finishes at dusk, when it is no longer safe to swing an axe, and makes his long way homeward by the wan light of the moon.

My farmer neighbour has passed an ordinary winter's day as winter days go here in Medonte. As he swings through the gap in the stone fence on the hill above his home, he admits to himself that he is glad that it is over. His sigh of relief, as he turns in at his own gate, is a heart-warming thing. He has earned his rest. All he has to do now is thaw out the pump, which is still frozen, or cut a new hole in the ice of the creek, which has frozen over again. The cattle are thirsty again. The horses are thirsty again. All are hungry again. Hay and straw must be pitched down out of the mow again, and oats, chop, meal, and grain measured out to all. And there is the milking . . .

"But, pshaw," says the farmer, as he stands up his skis in a snow bank by the kitchen door. "Chores aren't work. No . . . A farmer works all day and rests while choring."

He smiles at his wife, who waves to him from the kitchen window, and goes on down the yard to the barn.

# PART 4

## Interrupted Eden

*I built my house where waters run*
*And silent cedars thank the sun*

*Where lilies bob and small trout play*
*And peace seemed settled down to stay*

*Where under ancient apple trees*
*Goats stood in daisies to their knees*

*I built and dreamed and this my fate*
*To shoulder arms and lock the gate.*

K.M.W. 1941

# 10

*We Hang Up a Dream*

LUCY AND I HAD DREAMED THAT WE WERE THROUGH WITH cities. We overlooked the possibility that the cities of the world might not be through with us. We spent the long winter evenings planning our spring campaign. When the snow went, we made a lawn out of the sand and wood chips that our builders had left in front of the house. We laid a flagstone walk, put up a rail fence, and laid out a flower garden. We began the building of a studio. And then the stinking black fog which had spread out of the German city of Berlin, to infect every city in the world, reached even to Moonstone Creek. I hung up a dream with my overalls.

Four years is a long time to leave a live dream hanging on a hook. Time dragged. The new uniform that I had worn out of the Owl Pen the day I kissed Lucy good-bye, grew thin and shabby. So did my hair. So did certain stained and dog-eared photographs in my wallet. It seemed, as the months grew into years, that the war would never end. Suddenly it did. I stopped drawing plans for chicken houses on the backs of secret documents, became ill, and headed for home.

To dream for years of home, to serve one's time abroad and then, at long last, to come home, that surely is heaven on earth; enough for any soldier. It was for me, I know, the day that I at last turned in again past a weathered wooden gate to where a gray timber house nestled behind a screen of cedar trees. I don't remember getting out of the car. I do remember standing beside it, with my mouth open, unable to speak.

I was home again. This was the Owl Pen. The thought whirred like a rocket in my mind. This was no photograph. This was the real thing, real earth, and wood, and stone. The gate we had opened I had hung. The post it swung on I had planted. The crooked rail fences on either side of it I had piled. I had worked with Lucy making the lawn we stood on. I had watched her, years before, planting the great-grandfathers of the flowers that bloomed beside us. I could hear creek water laughing over the stones in the valley behind the house. Everything was as it should be. Everything was the same.

Hand in hand, Lucy and I walked up the winding flagstone path to the old timber house. Its mellow timbers had seen many a home-coming, I had no doubt. There had been other wars than this one since they had been cut out of the bush. I noticed that the mortar chinking was falling away from between some of the timbers, and that yawning cracks had opened around some of the window frames. The wooden boxes around the cellar windows were rotten, and there were wide checks in the oaken threshold board. A streak of dull, red rust ran down from the iron thumb latch over the green paint of the door. The war years had left their mark on the old house, too.

Inside, everything was like a new pin. Lucy had been busy there. The red birch floor shone with polish. The antique pewter that I had sent home from England glinted softly in the late afternoon sunlight that slanted through the small-paned windows on to the black oak dresser where they stood. The heavy beams of the ceiling glistened with new oil. Lined up, like soldiers I thought wryly, against the honey-brown pine of the walls, stood the hundreds of old books that I had haggled for in the dusty second-hand shops of England and Scotland.

"Well?" said Lucy.

"Well!" said I.

What else was there to say? This was my heaven on earth, my Eden, and I was in it. I was happy. There was only one lack. I missed the sudden thrust of a shaggy grey head between my arm and side, the thrust of Stormy, our Irish wolfhound, demanding her need of attention. Stormy had died while I was away, and was buried under the daisies and bloodroot, within sight of the trout-haunted stream she had loved so well. I missed her, but I did not mention her for I did not want to cloud the day for Lucy, and I still had the crazy feeling that I would come upon her, in the next room, or down the path, or over the hill. If dogs have souls, Stormy is still at Owl Pen.

In the country, need does not wait on sentiment. Within an hour of my home coming I was digging to uncover a septic tank and find out what was wrong with the plumbing. Actually, we had no time to waste. It was late summer. If we were to have bees and chickens, and ducks in the spring, we had to make ready for them now. We had to repair, alter, and enlarge existing buildings. We had to build new ones. We had to level ground and lay sod. We had to dig up and bury tile. We had to put up new fences, and pull old fences down. We had to find materials and labour. Winter was just over the horizon, and winter was our dead-line. If we failed to finish before freeze-up, our entire programme would be put back another year. It had already been put back four. We went to work.

After a four-year sleep, the Owl Pen awoke to life. The song of the creek was lost once again in the roar of trucks, the clank of many tools, and the shouts of workmen. Lucy was time-keeper and bookkeeper. I strode about, the perfect foreman, attempting to get a perfect job done, and failing miserably. We had been unable to get our old carpenters back. They were far afield, on other jobs, working for wages that we could not afford to pay. The men we did hire as carpenters called themselves carpenters. They had hammers and saws.

We set a high standard at Owl Pen. Our century-old home had been built, and re-built, by master craftsmen, and we wanted the new work to match. It didn't. I ordered work torn down and re-done. I moaned over wasted materials and wasted time. On pay days Lucy and I moaned together over the pay cheques we wrote. Pride in craftsmanship seemed vanished from the earth.

Something had to be done, either to slow down the cash out-go, or speed up the work, and that something had to be done soon. I was at my wit's end when one sunny afternoon a farmer neighbour dropped in and stood watching the work in progress.

"What do you think?" I asked.

"Well . . ."

"Go on, say it!"

"Well . . . " He filled his pipe slowly. "Well, it's nice to be rich."

"Good heavens, man, I'm not rich!"

"Well . . . " He lit his pipe, "you act like it." His pipe gurgled. "Still, you're city folk. I'm a farmer. If it was me, I'd be doing the job myself, and keeping the cash for beasts, seeds, and other needments."

"But . . ."

"Years ago," continued the old farmer implacably, "years ago my dad wrote some good advice for us up on the big beam in the barn. The writing's still there, plain as day. It says:

If you'd pass the old homestead on to your son;
    Do it yourself, don't hire it done."

He coughed, and put another match to his pipe.

"But I couldn't . . . " I protested, "I wouldn't know how to begin . . . "

The farmer smiled dryly, "No, I don't reckon so. Still, it strikes me some of the men you're paying don't know so much about some things either."

For days I mulled over my farmer neighbour's advice. It was friendly advice, good advice, essential to successful country living. I know that now, but I was, at the time, afraid to act on it. Lucy went to town for groceries. I went into the house, telephoned my bank, asked for my bank balance, and then went down among the creek-side cedars for ten minutes' silent communion with worms and other low forms of animal life. I came out of the cedars to be met, as chance would have it, by a workman who wanted more pay. That settled it.

When Lucy came back from town there were no carpenters, no masons, no workmen of any kind to be seen at Owl Pen. The only man on the place was her husband, draped in a carpenter's apron, armed with a hammer, and seated astride the honey house roof. He was talking to himself. He was telling somebody that she couldn't see, apparently a farmer neighbour, or the ghost of one, that

he was right, dead-right. He was telling the world. Every
once in awhile he would raise his hammer above his head
and shake it at the unoffending branches of a near-by pine.
Lucy listened for awhile, and then went quietly into the
house. She put on a second carpenter's apron that was there,
and picked up another hammer.

Lucy joined me on the honey house roof. She joined
me on the garage roof, and on the brooder house roof. She
dug. She lugged. She split and pounded. As the days and
weeks passed, her hands became rough and scratched, and
her nails broken. About her there lingered the fragrance of
tar and turpentine. When she reached into her pocket for
a lipstick she had to dig through shavings and shingle nails
to find it. She worked beside me ten hours a day, seven days
a week. She did all the work that might have been expected
of a strong man, and she did it well. Without her, I would
have failed utterly.

The going was not easy, even when our farmer neighbours,
realizing better than we did that we had bitten off more than
we could chew, neglected their own pressing tasks to give us
the occasional helping hand. When a flurry of hail caught
us working with blued lips and numbed hands on the garage
walls, a countryman living about two miles away just
happened by. He stayed a week. When we made ready to
attempt the impossible and do our bee-yard grading with
shovel and wheel-barrow, the owner of a neighbouring farm
turned his team in at our gate. We did our last big job of
the year, that of sodding the bee-yard, in an unending rain
that froze as it fell and turned the turf into dripping bundles
of congealing mud.

Big jobs gave way to little jobs, to a multitude of important
little jobs. We raced at them. Tempers grew short and thin.
The days clanged by. We prayed each evening that winter
would come, that snow and frost would come, and write a
finish to such slavery. We prayed each morning for just

one more good working day. We tumbled into bed each night with every muscle aching, too tired to sleep.

At last there came a morning when we got up to find that our world was wrapped in white. Snow was everywhere, inches deep, and still falling. Once again the big birch tree behind the house was as I remembered it of old, a magical scrawl of black and silver against a stormy sky. Winter had come at last. Finish was written at last to our outside work. We did not care. The race was won.

A fine honey-house, resplendent with paint and whitewash stood in the valley. Beside it was a trim brown and white storage shed. Nearby was the bee-yard, level, and under the snow, green with sod. To the south of the Owl Pen, behind a bright new fence, stood a tiny brooder house, complete even to litter and brooder stove. A new garage stood bravely by the road, and a newly completed lean-to against the east end of the house held all our surplus gear. The Owl Pen itself had been re-chinked and stained and painted. We were ready for winter, ready for spring, ready we thought, for whatever might come. We both sighed deeply. Strangely enough we felt almost sorry that the rush was over.

We had actually enjoyed it all.

# 11

## *We Meet a Pig*

THE STORK, OR WHATEVER IT IS THAT BRINGS BABY PIGS
into Medonte in the winter time, was late, days late, in
coming to Plum Tree Farm. He should have arrived 114
days to the minute from the time that Gertrude, Farmer
Jim's big pink sow, decided to have a family. He didn't.
All day long Jim watched Gertrude storm about her straw-
filled pen, grumbling and grunting, resenting the delay,
growling unmentionable things. Jim fed her hot slops, and
scratched her belly, but still the stork that brings little pigs
stayed away from Plum Tree Farm.

That night Jim kept a lighted lantern beside his bed, and
slept in his clothes. There was a chance that they might
arrive in the darkness, and with no one around to help, in
such cold and windy weather, anything might happen.
Gertrude was a young sow, and this was to be her first litter.
Three times during the night Jim got up, picked up his
lantern, and struggled out through the snow drifts to the
barn. Three times Gertrude grunted her appreciation, and
eyed the light. Three times the cattle bawled, begging for
food. Three times the barn cat meowed and rubbed against
his frosty legs, begging for milk. There were no baby pigs.

The 115th day was the 114th all over again. Once again
through the long dark hours of a winter's night a lantern
burned at Plum Tree Farm, and once again Jim spent the
night wading, every three hours, through the piled up drifts
between the house and barn. Gertrude had just about
wrecked her pen by now. She had torn her trough apart
and eaten part of the lumber that it had been made of. She

had stamped and ripped her straw bedding into chaff. She had butted two boards in the pen doors loose, and rooted a foot-deep hole in the floor. She was no happier than Jim.

The 116th day was a golden day, mild and sunny, with tall white plumes of steam rising from the south side of the barn roof towards a June-like sky. The snow drifts shone like mounded diamonds. It was too good a day to waste waiting for pigs that never came. Farmer Jim hitched his horse to the black cutter.

"I'm cutting wood with dad to-day," he told Alice his wife.

"But . . . " protested Alice.

"If I'm needed, telephone," said Jim, and was gone.

Alice was worried. It did not seem reasonable to her that, in this day and age, storks, any more than trains, should run so outrageously behind schedule. She spoiled her bread, trying to watch it and Gertrude at the same time. By noon the sow seemed stark, staring mad.

"Hawg wild," said Alice to Jim, on the telephone. "Rampaging like a devil . . . Restless as sin . . . You'd better come home."

"I'll be home at supper time," said Jim.

"Gertrude will beat you to it."

"Maybe . . . "

"What will I do?"

"Nothing," replied Jim, "nothing at all. It's a nice day, and Gertrude will know what to do without you butting in."

"But . . . "

"I figger I'll be home in time," said Jim, and went back to his chopping in the bush.

The sun was like a red apple on the western rim of hills when the cutter, bearing Jim and his father, came down the snow piled concession line, and turned in at Plum Tree Farm. They seemed in no hurry as they unhitched the horse and led it to stable. They brought it oats and hay, and put a couple of forksful of fresh straw into its stall. They put the cutter away in a corner of the yard, smoked a pipeful of tobacco, and peered in through the hen house window at the fat hens clucking there. Jim patted his collie dog.

"He's a good dog," he said to his father.

"He's learned a lot from mine," said the father to his son.

Together they studied the western sky, and debated the prospects of continuing good weather. Then they knocked out their pipes, stamped the hissing embers into the snow, and opened the barn door. They went in, to find Gertrude, her small eyes bulging with unbelief and sheer amazement, studying a minute but perfect replica of herself that writhed in the straw at her feet. Jim, his father, the stork, and Gertrude's first-born, had come into the barn together.

Farmer Jim picked up the baby pig, wrapped it in a burlap feed bag, and carried it out of the barn, across the barn yard, into the farm house kitchen where Alice put it into a stove-warmed wash tub that she had lined with several thicknesses of newsprint. During the next three quarters of an hour he made several such trips.

"I wonder how many there will be," pondered Alice.

"I don't know," responded her husband, slowly rolling himself a cigarette, and surveying the babies with shining eyes. "I don't know at all. I'll be satisfied with eight or nine. Any more than that and I'll be just plain tickled to death."

The wash tub filled to overflowing. A copper boiler was called into service. Still the little pigs kept coming, in two's and three's, from the barn into the kitchen in the arms of Farmer Jim. At last there was a pause.

"Eleven," counted Alice. "Maybe that is all she is going to have."

As she spoke, the door opened again. Jim was back again with two more squirming little bundles of pinkness in his arms. He dropped them into the boiler and went out again.

"Thirteen," exclaimed Alice. "I do hope that is the lot. Gertrude's only able to look after eleven. She's only got eleven tits. This means that I've got to bring up two myself . . . keep them by the kitchen stove here . . . and a kitchen does get cluttered up. She studied them for a moment, and then smiled. "Still, I don't mind, I guess. Baby pigs are cute little things," she looked up. "Ain't they now?"

Indeed they were. Only an hour old, and clean as a whistle, the little pigs in the wash tub and boiler were storming about in a frantic, never ceasing, whirligig of motion. They were thrusting everywhere with their ridiculously small pink satin snouts, seeking the food which instinct told them should be at hand in warm abundance. They nuzzled each other. They sucked the newspaper of their wash tub pen into shreds, and with their razor-sharp little teeth, polished the copper sides of the boiler until it shone. They squealed with disappointment and rage, and explored the lamp-lit brilliance of the outer world with staring, beady eyes.

"That's the lot," said Jim, coming in with his lantern, which he blew out and set down by the door.

"Thank goodness for that," sighed Alice, and then, "mustn't be too long getting them back to their mother."

"After supper," said Jim, and turning his back on the thirteen little pigs, sat down at the lamp-lit table.

Some folk like music with their meals. After a busy day they find comfort and relaxation in sitting down to dinner in a room that is filled with the crying of muted violins, or the hushed throb of an organ. Alice and Jim, and Lucy and I, found equally pleasing and soul satisfying, the healthful pigmy wailing of the thirteen little pigs that scrutted and rustled in crumpled newsprint in the boiler and tub by the stove. We sat down to boiled eggs, home-made bread, tea, and raisin pie, with the music of the spheres in our ears, the music of new life. The dainty pink bodies squirming and tumbling over each other a yard from the table's edge were to us, as we passed the dishes, poetry in motion, more meaningful than those that tumble each night in the floor shows presented to tired city diners—more meaningful, and thirteen times more useful.

"Mustn't be too long getting them back to their mother," prompted Alice, when supper was done.

"After I've done the chores," grinned Jim, and picking up his mitts and lighting his lantern, went out into the night.

When Jim came back into the room a short half-hour later, he found it filled with people. His father had come back up from the neighbouring farm. A couple had arrived from the corner store, bringing with them the corn syrup needed by Alice to feed the two little pigs that were to be her special care. There was Lucy and myself, Alice and the thirteen pigs, and it was a small room. Jim looked about him, grinned again, and sat down to a cigarette.

"Mustn't be too long . . . " began Alice.

"Time for a smoke," said Jim, and turned to his father. "A nice lot of little pigs."

"I dunno," replied the older man, but those closest to him saw him smile behind his upraised hand. "Two of the lot are small." He paused, and then as Jim opened his mouth to voice an outraged protest on behalf of his livestock. "You've got a nice lot of pigs, Jim."

That, from one farmer to another, is a compliment, an important compliment indeed.

There remained a few things to be done. The bloody little cord trailing untidily from the belly of each pigling had to be cut off close to the body, and Jim did this with Alice's sewing scissors. Four needle-sharp milk teeth had to be cut out of each tiny jaw, and Jim did this with a pair of rusty pliers. The wee pigs protested mightily, filling the room with a shrill squealing that seemed all out of proportion to their small lungs.

"Gotta do it," explained Jim. "If it ain't done, the old pig won't let them suck. They hurt her tits." He continued his work with the pliers as he spoke. "If she does let them suck,"—snip went a tooth—"they spoil her for more litters,"—snip went another tooth—"tit goes blind,"—snip—"no milk"—snip. Snip. Snip. "Often wonder how wild pigs get along." Snip. "Maybe they don't have these dirty black milk-teeth."

The job was done. Jim gathered up the tiny black teeth and put them into the kitchen stove. The little pigs scrutted and raced again in the tattered newsprint, seeking again for food.

"We must get them back to their mother," protested Alice once again. "If we keep them away from her too long the old devil will like as not refuse to take them at all."

"They've been away long enough, Jim," put in the older man.

"I know it," returned Jim with a broad smile, and very deliberately put on his mitts, and picked up the pig-filled wash tub. "They're going home to mama now." He looked around him at the crowd in the little farm house kitchen, "If you folks are coming too, one of you might carry the lantern, and another of you might bring the wash boiler." He chuckled. "We'll make a queer procession through the barnyard this night."

Gertrude was very glad to get her babies back. The look of complacent happiness on her heavy face as she welcomed Jim into the pen, was almost comical to see. Yet, somehow, it wasn't. It was, instead, rather touching. Jim poured the piglets, first out of the wash tub, and then out of the boiler, into the straw beside her. She grunted happily, and lay down on her side. Her babies flowed towards her, as inevitably, as naturally, as a river to the sea. In a few minutes all were feeding noisily, happily. The sow grunted her contentment. Jim, on his knees beside her, looked up. He, too, was content.

# 12

## *We Endure a Thaw*

I HAVE NO DOUBT THAT THE WEATHER SUITED GERTRUDE. The thaw that sank our world in an unseasonable flood of mud and slush, and brown flood water, must have been a lovely thing, from her point of view, but Lucy and I did not like it. Neither did our neighbours. We were glum, all of us. Our spirits went down as the temperature went up. We neither gambolled nor whistled. We slithered and sploshed. We sniffed the warm air and found cold comfort in the fact that sooner or later winter would come into her own again, decent snow would again cover the naked fields, the roads would drift and close again, and water would freeze again at nights in the kettle on the back of the stove.

An unseasonable thaw of any duration can be, to a countryman, something approaching a major disaster. It touches his food supply, his fuel supply, his buildings, his transport, his work, his bank account, and his peace of mind. In the country, winter living and winter economy is based on the assumption that there will be snow, and that there will be frost, and that both will be more or less constant between the months of December and March. When they are not, there is the devil to pay.

At the Owl Pen, our first concern was our meat supply. Taking a leaf from the notebook of our farmer neighbours, we had, like them, stocked up for the winter. We had purchased a dozen fat hens, four ducks, and a trio of geese, a quarter of beef, and a quarter of pork, and hung the lot in a solemn row in the new lean-to at the end of the house.

They froze so hard that when we wanted a joint or a steak, we had to tackle the carcasses with an axe and cross-cut saw. As a prelude to dressing a chicken or duck, we had to hang the bird, for a day at least, in the warm stove corner in the kitchen. We didn't mind. Meat keeps forever that way.

Then came the thaw. The frost came out of everything. Our meat supply grew soft and flabby. Then it grew moist, and began to drip slow drops of blood and water on to the lean-to floor. We watched it with panic in our eyes. The thaw persisted, our meat began to darken. We dragged an old apple barrel out of the cellar, rubbed our poultry, beef and pork with salt, and then packed it in snow, which we had to search for in the darkest fastness of our neighbour's wood-lot, and drag home in a box. This in January! Our next concern was for our new cement work, the piers and foundations under our new buildings, the new cement floor in the honey house. Water ran in torrents down the hillside, lapping our piers and foundations as though they were the buttresses of a dock. We grabbed picks and shovels and dug and ditched, like a pair of ground-hogs gone mad.

Our neighbours had their troubles, too. Mountains of turnips, which they had piled in the corners of the stables as winter feed for their cattle, grew soft and mushy as the thaw persisted. Thousands of pale green and anaemic red sprouts appeared in the piles. The owners watched this new life glumly, knowing that as the sprouts grew they sucked the goodness out of the roots. Cabbages hung in long brown rows from the ceiling beams in the cattle byre, and used to brighten the winter ration in the chicken house, grew black with rot.

As the rushing snow water invaded the swamps and bushlands, all work stopped there, and woodsmen sat idly at home, unable to earn the dollars needed, and counted upon, to pay for next spring's seeds. A man can't cut fence posts in a swamp where the water is waist deep. Trucks can't pick up saw-logs, or cord-wood, in a bushlot that is swimming axle deep in water and bumper-deep in mud. On the lowlands, only the muskrats were happy. They, excited by the spring-like rush of water, gambolled from half-submerged stump to half-submerged fence, like little brown elves gone mad. Warm, wet days dragged by.

Then, as suddenly as it had come, the thaw left us. A freezing wind soughed in the pines. A flurry of snow-laden wind hid the elm trees. Vagrant winter, the unabashed hussy, came again to our hills. A blizzard piled nearly four feet of snow on the lee side of the Owl Pen roof. Moonstone Creek disappeared completely. So did the little ravine it ran in. Snow filled it level with the concession line, and left no mark at all to tell a traveller which was road and which was gully or field. Lucy and I, having no horses to drag us through the drifts, and no skis to carry us over them, were as completely cut off from the outside world as was Robinson Crusoe on his desert island.

We didn't care. Our cupboards were full. Our wood pile was a big one. Our meat supply was frozen hard again. Our radio gave us news and music, and we had our books. We had enough work to keep us busy every day, all day, until spring came round again, or the township fathers decided to let the township snow-plough, the existence of which we had almost come to doubt, wander into our corner of the municipality.

Lucy's studio, ordinarily given over to wood-carving and sculpture, was our workshop. It swallowed white paint by the gallon, tar by the quart, putty by the five-pound can, nails by the box full and wire by the mile, as we worked on the bits and pieces that were to furnish our bee-yard. Every day saw a few more hive bodies, a few more supers, a few more covers, stands, or frames, completed, and added to the growing pile in the store shed.

We were happy in our isolation and our work, happier even than Gertrude, who lay snugly with her eleven piglings, in deep straw in her pen at **Plum Tree Farm**. After all, what more can two people ask of life than this; to stand in a warm workshop, with their backs to a blazing fire, working on bee-hives while wind-driven snow spatters the window panes. To work on bee-hives is to dream of spring, to hear in the wall-muffled humming of the winter blast the drone of pollen-dusty honey-bees drifting from flower to flower.

# PART 5

# Murder is Wholesale

*The Rabbit has a charming face;*
*Its private life is a disgrace.*
*I really dare not name to you*
*The awful things that rabbits do;*
*Things that your paper never prints—*
*You only mention them in hints,*
*They have such lost, degraded souls*
*No wonder they inhabit holes . . .*

ANON. (20TH CENT.)

# 13

*We Sit Up With Chicks*

THERE WAS PEACE AT THE OWL PEN, THE SORT OF PEACE
that comes inevitably in the winter time, to an old log house
by a singing creek, with deep snow all around. Our living
was a song, sung in time to the soft sighing of wind in the
pine trees, to the gentle murmuring of dark water, and
the swish of northern lights. We drew our patchwork quilt
up under our chins each night with the thought that if
paradise was not like Owl Pen, someone in heaven had
slipped.

Then, suddenly, there was no peace. Peace hoisted her
skirts, and showed her legs, and went over the furthest
hill. She cleared out of Owl Pen, and out of Moonstone
Valley. Peace, it seemed, was allergic to poultry, especially
baby poultry, and most especially to baby poultry in the

hands of amateur poultrymen. Lucy and I awoke from
our dreaming to the harsh reality of the fact that like
Jericho, which had been tumbled by a bugle toot, our
paradise was being shivered by a peep.

To look at a baby chick, a pathetically small handful of
dainty yellow fluff, is to wonder how this could be. The
wee mite weighs much less than the egg it came from. It
has a beak no larger than a plump grain of wheat, two
feet that can be hidden under a postage stamp, legs like
pins, and wings so fine and small as to make those of a
butterfly seem gross by comparison. It is so delicate that
a sudden change in temperature, of even a few degrees,
will kill it. Cold food or drinking water will cause it to
lie down and die. A hammer dropped beside it on the
board it is standing on will jar it into eternity. Speak
harshly to it, and it will lose weight. And yet it is, as every
farmer knows, and as we so quickly found out, a mighty
atom that can blast all peace and quietness out of a man's
life.

Actually, it was the mere thought of a baby chick's many
weaknesses that sent peace skadaddling out of our valley.
Word came that our baby chicks, some three hundred of
them, were on their way to us from a Trappist Monastery
in Quebec where they had been hatched. They were very
special chicks, Chanticler chicks, a distinctively Canadian
breed of poultry which had been developed in the monastery by one of the monks, Brother Wilfred, and they were
to be the first of their kind to come into our part of the
world.

When word of their impending arrival reached us, we
looked out of the Owl Pen window at the concession line,
filled to the fence tops, as they had been for two long weeks
past, with drifted snow. The weather was cold. Unless
the roads were ploughed, the only way we could get our
chicks home from the distant railroad station would be by

horse and sleigh. We had visions of their arrival after such a long slow trip, white with frost, and frozen stiff.

A dozen times a day, for days on end, I hung on the telephone, pestering council members, reeve and deputy-reeve, and township clerk, in an effort to get our road ploughed out so that our chicks might come to us in a fast and heated automobile. I got promises, but no plough. I pleaded; I threatened; I got excuses. The ploughs were at the west end of the township. Could they be brought back? Sorry, they were trying to buck open a road in order to get a sick woman to the hospital. Could they come back when that was done? Sorry, the ploughs were broken down. I did not inquire into the truth or untruth of a rumour which had it that one of the ploughs was stuck in the reeve's lane.

Some day, I am going to run for public office in Medonte. I want some day to be in a position to fire whoever it is that was responsible for sending a snow plough bumping down the side-road to within a quarter of a mile of the Owl Pen, then to turn tail and flee back into oblivion. After all our trouble, we were left still that distance of bottomless snow drifts between us and the end of a clear motor road. If there is such a thing as mental telepathy, ears burned in Medonte that night. The thermometer stood at zero.

We really needn't have worried at all. It is apparently true that fate tempers the wind to the shorn lamb. The fatal day, the day our chicks were due to arrive, dawned with a burst of golden sunshine, and a wind from the south that sent the mercury shooting up its little glass thermometer tube. The air filled with the cawing of north-bound crows. The roads ran water. The snow left the hills, and the hillside fields. Spring, and our chicks, it seemed, were arriving together.

Lucy and I walked down to the corners, through sodden, shrinking drifts, to where the ploughed road ended. A friend in need was bringing our chicks that far in the heated

cab of his truck. We sat by the roadside and waited, Lucy
with an eiderdown comforter on her knees, and I with a
camel's hair motor rug on mine. We heard the distant
hoot of a train whistle. A thin wisp of black smoke drifted
into the sky from the valley on the far side of our northern
rim of hills. Our train was pulling into distant Eady Station. Soon . . . soon . . . Jean and Anne White, two little
girls from a neighbouring hilltop farm, joined us with their
hand-sleighs. We were not to want for either transport or
help. The minutes dragged by.

"Perhaps the truck is in the ditch," I hazarded impatiently.

"It is eight miles from the station, the way it has to come,"
pointed out Lucy.

"Maybe the chicks didn't arrive," I dithered, after another ten minutes of restless waiting. "Maybe the truck
didn't meet the train."

Lucy grinned, lit a cigarette, and pointed. Down the
road, past the long row of great elms that mark our corners,
came Joe in his little blue truck. He bumped and slithered
over the ice the thaw had laid bare. He splashed through
thaw water. Joe, who always seems to be coming to our
rescue, had done it again. On the driver's seat beside him,
were three big cardboard boxes. Our chicks! A steamy
gust of hot air rushed into our faces as we opened the cab
door. A full orchestra of shrill peeping made bedlam.

"It's August in here," grinned Joe, wiping his red face
with the back of his glove and pointing at the car heater.
"Must be ninety in the shade. The chicks aren't wearing
heavy underwear like me. They love it."

I don't think we even said "good-day" to Joe. We took
our precious boxes out of the cab, piled them on the hand
sleigh, wrapped them in the eiderdown robe and the camel's
hair rug, and fled back down our concession line at a full
gallop. I'm sure we didn't say "Good-bye" or "Thank-

you". We simply grabbed our chicks and ran for home, I pulling, Jean and Anne pushing, and Lucy mounting guard over the wrappings, which continually tangled with the runners of the speeding sleigh. We looked back once to see Joe, standing alone in the middle of the roadway, watching us. He seemed to be shaking. Something seemed to be amusing him. He waved us on with both hands, and on we went, peep-peep, puff-puff, splash-splash, all the way home.

We arrived safely with our load at the brooder house. All had been prepared, days in advance, for the event. The brooder stove was burning merrily. The thermometer stood at 95 degrees under the huge steel hover that surrounded it. Another thermometer, on the wall of the house, read 75 degrees. Strategically placed around the stove were feeder troughs, filled with a ground mixture of a dozen different grains, minerals, fish oils, milk powder, meat scrap, and assorted vitamins. Between the troughs were ranged a half-dozen water fountains, filled with sparkling warm water. The floor was spread with sand, and straw, and finally a thick layer of newsprint. No three hundred chicks ever had a more auspicious, a more luxurious, start in life.

Our first task was to make sure that every one of our little peepers had a drink. Finding needed utensils in short supply, Lucy raided our living room and brought out an antique pewter wine flagon, and a silver pitcher. From these we poured fresh water into china bowls, reminding ourselves as we did so, to buy galvanized pails the next time we were in town. Then we took our baby chicks, one by one, and dunked their protesting little heads, the whole three hundred of them, into the warm water. So our babies had their first drink on this earth. So they learned what their beaks and gullets were for. So they learned what water was, and what a nice drink it can be. So we learned what a horrible horde three hundred baby chicks can be.

Long before we had finished with the third boxful of

birds, the erstwhile contents of the first two had made themselves completely at home in their new world. They ranged about the water fountains like seasoned topers. They lined up at the mash troughs like aldermen at a free dinner. They scratched enthusiastically, instinctively, at the bare newsprint, two strokes with one leg, then three with the other, in perfect imitation of something they had never seen, a grown hen on a lawn. They played tag, cops-and-robbers, and who's-got-the-worm, with each other, racing around the brooder stove like a flock of downy meteors. They were healthy, happy, and content.

And yet they were, for all their prettiness, bloody-minded devils. Even as we watched the little blighters, but a few minutes out of their cardboard prison, Lucy had to reach out and rescue a spread-eagled little victim from the beaks of several would-be executioners. His sin was that he was a shade darker than the rest, and had a small drop of oil or other matter, caked on the small of his back. A few minutes later, another perky youngster who had injured his foot, ever so slightly, in transit, was attacked. Before we noticed his plight and took him up, his feet had been picked into a raw and bleeding pulp. All the nails were missing from his toes. His toes were mere stumps. Departure from the norm, we were to learn, is no more tolerated in a brooder house than it is in a small town. Our chicks were almost human in their viciousness.

We established an infirmary in a cardboard box back of the stove in the Owl Pen kitchen, and to it we each day carried the broken and maimed that we were able to rescue from the fury of their fellows. Those we were too late in rescuing, the tattered dead, I also carried to the kitchen, and despite Lucy's frantic protests, cremated in the kitchen stove.

It quickly became apparent that if we were to keep an adequate check on the welfare of our chicks, the brooder house would have to be visited every three hours, day and night. There were the injured to be rescued, the dead to be removed, the stove to be shaken and filled, and the temperature to be maintained. Feeders and water fountains had to be cleaned, filled and re-filled. At night the chicks, all of which seemed determined to sleep crowded together in piled-up heaps that brought suffocation and death to the undermost, had to be spread out evenly under the hover. Such chick deviltries as cannibalism, toe-picking, and feather pulling had to be watched for and dealt with. Every three hours, day and night, night and day . . .

It was a pleasant enough task at three o'clock in the afternoon; at three o'clock in the morning it was a horrible experience. It was something damnable. Every night, five minutes after I got to sleep, or so it seemed, I would have to suddenly charge out of my bed and leap through the icy darkness of the bedroom in an effort to shut off the exploding alarm clock before it awoke Lucy too. I never succeeded quite, but I tried.

While she lay snugly in bed, sleepily chuckling at my muffled profanity, I would pull trousers and rubber boots on over my pyjamas, light my lantern, and rumble away down the dark stairs to the deserted living room, and out through the snow to the brooder house. Invariably I would stumble off the path and find my way into the deepest drift on the place. Invariably the snow would pile over my boot tops and work its way down over my sockless, shuddering feet. Invariably I would arrive at the brooder house door muttering maledictions against all chickdom. Invariably our chicks, the stove, and the temperature would be all right. Invariably I would waste more minutes of precious sleeping time squatting in the warm, lantern-lit darkness of the brooder house talking crazy baby chick talk to the pretty little things, and falling in love with them all over again.

# 14

## *We Kill Them With Kindness*

OUR BOOKS ALL SAID, AND LUCY AND I IN OUR INEXPERI-
ence were utterly dependent upon our books, that the secret
of success in the brooding of chicks was maintenance of an
absolutely correct temperature in the brooder house. It
must not vary either up or down, so much as three degrees
a day, the books said. Lucy and I read, and Lucy and I
were impressed.

"Above all else, avoid chilling," shouted the Books.

When we built our brooder house we kept our reading
in mind. We decided that it should be so built and fitted
as to make chilling impossible. We put a double wooden
floor in it and laid thick asphalt felt between the floors. We
built the walls of inch-lumber on scantlings, covered them
with asphalt felt and covered the felt with cedar shingles.
We lined it inside with more inch-lumber and stuffed the
air space with a mixture of shavings and lime. We hung
double doors and arranged the window ventilation so that
no hint of direct draft could ever reach the floors. We
then, to make doubly sure that our chicks would have
ample hover space and ample heat, installed a stove and
brooder of 1,000 chick capacity. The house was a three
hundred chick house.

All might have gone well if March had come in like a
lion. Had the temperature dropped to at least 40 degrees
below zero, our brooder house would have functioned perfectly. But the temperature did not go down. It went up,
and up, and up. March was a nasty little lamb. The thermometer by the Owl Pen door registered summer heat.

The thermometer in the brooder house exploded. Its limit was 120 degrees.

Our chicks stopped playing. They stopped eating. They grew dull, listless, and dopey. Some lay down and would not get up. Some died. The cardboard infirmary back of the kitchen stove filled to overflowing. Lucy and I rushed for hammers and saws. We cut pieces out of the brooder house window. We drilled long rows of holes in the doors. We propped open the check drafts on the stove, and propped up the hover. We sat for hours on end with red faces and sweaty backs in the still torrid heat of our too-good brooder house, studying our tiny charges and picking up invalids. Twelve of them died in our hands. We felt like murderers.

I do not think there is anything on earth quite so limp, so pathetically limp, as a dead baby chick. It is such a finely made, fragile little thing, so soft and lovely in its yellow down. Had Lucy and I had been the sensible practical folk that we are not, we would have killed every single one of our surviving chicks and ordered a new lot. All our books insisted that after such an overheating they would never thrive, but always be sickly and liable to every kind of disease and infection imaginable. We shut our books. We couldn't do it.

Slowly, ever so slowly, the temperature in the brooder house went down. Down to 110 degrees crawled the silver thread in the glass tube of the new thermometer that we had hung by the hover. Down to 100 degrees, down, down to 95 degrees, the correct temperature. Our chicks still stood listlessly about, swaying a little on their pathetically little legs, many of them with eyes closed, many more with wee wings drooped. We had done what we could. We visited the brooder house again at six o'clock, and again at nine. There was no change.

At midnight, I awoke to the raucous roaring of the alarm clock. It was cold. The window curtains were blowing straight out from the open bedroom window and there was snow on the floor. March, having tired of playing sheep, was now trying to be a sheep-eater. I pulled on my rubber boots and my dressing-gown, and went out through the darkness to the brooder house. A bitter northwest wind raved in my face. A fine snow was sifting in through the holes we had bored in the brooder house door.

I was almost afraid to look at the tawny golden mat of little chicks spread under the hover, but look I had to do. I turned up the wick of my barn lantern and moved it closer. The yellow mat stirred and heaved as the light hit it. Here and there a little chick stood up. Here and there one peeped. As I watched, some of them moved from the hover to the water fountains. A dozen more made a bee-line for the feed troughs. The temperature under the hover was still correct, still 95 degrees. I turned the wick back down again, dimming the light. A shrill wail of protest filled the brooder house. It was a healthy wail. There was anger and hunger in it. I literally danced back through the snow to the Owl Pen. Our chicks were going to live, tra-la! Our chicks were going to live!

Lucy was awake when I went up to the bedroom, lying in the old spool bed, staring at the moonlit ceiling.

"How are they?" she asked, as I took off my dressing gown, kicked off my rubber boots, and shuddered into bed beside her.

"The chicks are . . . "

"Don't tell me if there are any more dead!"

"They are fine. The little devils are eating and drinking. They swore at me when I took the light away from them."

Lucy was silent a moment. "Ken . . . "

"Yes?"

"Somebody is going to say that it is lovely having such an early spring."

"Yes?"

"Yes, and somebody is going to get a punch on the nose."

# 15

## *We Hate Jack Rabbits*

WINTER WAS HAVING ITS LAST FLING. ONCE AGAIN THE
concession lines closed. Once again the bare, brown fields
disappeared under a mantle of snow. Sub-zero winds howled
through the pine trees. The elms on the hill-tops clattered their bare branches until they sounded like dancing
skeletons. We found starved dead birds in the snow. A
partridge that I shot was mere skin and bone. Lucy and I
got up one morning to find that rabbits, jack-rabbits, had
eaten the bark and branches from every one of our young
apple trees.

Of course it was our own fault. We should have wrapped
them in the autumn with burlap, or tar paper, or wire
mesh, but somehow, with a thousand and one other things
to be done before freeze-up, we never got around to it.
Now it was too late to do anything but stand in the snow
beside the murdered trees and plot the death of their
killers.

Guns, it seemed, were the thing. I went through the
mail order catalogue, picked a likely sort of weapon and
sent in my order. I do believe that the rabbits knew that
until that gun arrived, we were helpless to deal with them.
They haunted us. They literally thumbed their noses at
us. Morning after morning I saw them from our bedroom
window, cavorting on the snow-covered lawn, nibbling at
the skinned white corpses of our apple trees. I came upon
them crouched in the shadow of our wood pile; I stumbled
over them crouched in the sleigh ruts on the hillside when

I went for milk. I threw snowballs at them. Once I threw the milk.

The day the gun arrived rabbits vanished from the face of the earth. Though I hunted diligently over a mile of surrounding farmland, I could not find so much as a sign of them, a single dropping, or one fresh track. I tried again and again. Day after day I took my gun and ammunition and walked the fence rows. I got no rabbit.

"You're not the only one," comforted a neighbour. "My young lad has been hunting for jacks all winter, and he ain't got one yet. The other morning he was taking a short-cut across the corner field. It was snowing pretty hard. He saw a bump in the snow in front of him and thought it was a stone or something, so he gave it a kick, just curious like, and a jack-rabbit jumped three feet in the air in front of him. 'Course his gun was at home. Funny, eh?"

I didn't think so. Having trudged weary snow-filled miles through swamp, field, and bushland hunting for the blistering things, and finding none, I was not at all amused by his word picture of a school boy stumbling over one within forty yards of my own front door. I said so, and Lucy, who was in the kitchen making tea, choked strangely.

The next day another neighbour, one wise in the ways of our little back-stabbing, tree-girdling brothers of the wild, offered to go hunting with me. He would show me rabbits, he said.

"We've had one a week all winter," he boasted. "Getting tired of eating them at home."

So the next morning I went hunting with the expert. He showed me jack-rabbits all right, but the nearest we got to them as they legged it over the fields like long-eared lightning bolts, was a quarter of a mile.

"You'll just strain your gun trying to shoot them at that distance," he exclaimed disgustedly. "It's a caution how

wild they are. It does beat all! Why just the other day
I nearly drove the team over one of the creatures. It was
crouched beside the bush road, in plain view, and it didn't
budge an inch as I went by. I drove on, got my load, and
started back for home. The rabbit was in the same place,
and he still didn't move. As I drove past him, I just leaned
over the side of my seat and dropped a piece of cordwood
on him." He smacked his lips reminiscently. "Made tasty
eating, he did."

The rabbits were laughing at us. That night a great
hulking brute of a jack-rabbit chased Titch, the Owl
Pen cat, the length of our shovelled path from the roadway to our front door. Iron, as they say in the movie
magazines, entered my soul. No darned rabbit could do
that to our cat and get away with it. I would shoot
me a rabbit or else . . .

"Or else what?" inquired Lucy when I told her of my
determination to avenge our fruit trees and Titch. She
didn't seem impressed.

"You never can tell what your luck will be," put in my
farmer neighbour who was sitting by our fireplace with
his gun on his knees, ready to hunt with me again. "Why
just the other day a fellow who lives not too far from here
went out hunting. He hunted all day and never saw a
single thing, no fox, no rabbit, no nothing. We watched
him coming home down that side-hill field back of the barn
at Old Inn Farm. We were sitting on the fence. And what
do you think! Loping along behind him, not more than
twenty-five feet behind him, and right in his very foot-
prints, was the biggest jack-rabbit I ever did see."

"Maybe the rabbit that chased Titch last night followed
us home yesterday afternoon," I put in waggishly.

"Maybe you got home just in time," said Lucy with an
evil grin.

I did not deign to answer. I closed the door from the outside and headed slowly up the hill. I knew what the outcome of the day's hunting would be. So did Lucy. So, I think, did my companion trudging along silently behind me. As we crested the hill, he cleared his throat . . .

"Well?" I queried, knowing the signs.

"I was just thinking . . ."

"Yes . . ."

"Rabbits is the dangdest things."

We trudged on.

# PART 6

## The Song of the Manure Spreader

*I know two things about the horse*
*And one of them is rather coarse.*

Anon. (20th Cent.)

# 16

*We Make Maple Syrup*

IT DIDN'T MATTER A BIT TO LUCY AND ME THAT SNOW STILL covered the ground, that the ground was frozen, and that the mercury in the thermometer still huddled close to the bottom of its little glass tube. When a crow caws on a hillside, it is spring. Winter is over. It is time for sulphur and molasses, and time to get the rusty spiles and sap buckets down from the beams in the woodshed. It is maple syrup time.

Some folks say that there is an affinity between maple trees and crows, that the trees wait until the big black birds fly over before sending the sweet sugar-laden sap coursing up out of their buried roots into trunk and limb. Whatever modern science may say of this old belief, Lucy and I like to believe it true. It is a nice thought, and somehow, as one watches the crows cawing and flapping in the bright March sunlight over snow-covered fields, over sleeping woodlots, it is not hard to believe.

"Caw," say the crows, "caw-caw."

And the woods rustle as though awakening from a long sleep, and a pale hint of green glows in the bark of the willow and poplar trees.

"Caw-caw," say the crows again. "Caw-caw."

And buds swell on the birch trees, and on the elm trees, and a farmer standing with his axe beside a new gash in a maple tree trunk shouts suddenly to his son,

"Ho! John! Ho! Sap's runnin'! It's runnin' good!"

Then it is that the party lines go humming mad. The word goes out along the concession lines, down the side roads and across the township. Sap's runnin'! Runnin'! Runnin'! It's runnin' good. Then it is that all the youngling pigs, chicks, lambs and calves, until then first in every farmer's thoughts, take second place to the tall bare trees on the hillsides. Then it is that barns and farm houses empty of their men folk and of their women folk too. The life of the township concentrates in the woodlots.

It is an ancient chore, this maple syrup making. The first settlers in Medonte noted in their letters home that the Indians of the area cut deep V-shaped gashes into the rough bark of the micktan trees, as they called the maple trees, and put little troughs, which they scooped out of pith-hearted alder twigs, at the point of the gash. The "maple water" dripped from these crude spiles into scooped-out basswood logs, or birch-bark baskets. The sap was heated by dropping red-hot stones into it, and kept boiling by constantly replacing the stones until it became a thick syrup, a golden brown sugar, micktan sweet.

This heating of stones, and re-heating of stones, must have been a back-breaking task. Red faces must have grown redder during the long hours spent leaning over flaring wood fires. Dark eye-brows must have singed, and red fingers blistered as the glowing stones were hauled out of the blaze and lifted, with the help of a crotched branch, into the bulging baskets of steaming sap.

It takes some fifty gallons of sap to make a gallon of good syrup, and up to three gallons of syrup to make a pound of sugar. The production of a pound of the stuff must have taken the Indians long days of almost slave-like labour. It is not surprising that the pioneers noted that the Indians welcomed with outstretched hands, and thieving fingers, the iron kettles that the white men brought into the country with them. To be able to boil sap over the fire, to be able to throw the accursed heating stones into the nearest creek, must have delighted the Ojibway squaws beyond measure.

Thomas Meed tells of the redmen at Pidgeon Lake hiring kettles in 1835:

"As soon as the sap begins to rise, the squaws betake themselves in families, or select parties, to maple groves, or sugar bushes as they are called. There they erect a camp, and prepare troughs, and firewood, and collect all the kettles they can borrow or hire in the neighbourhood. This done they begin to tap the trees with a tomahawk, inserting a tube in each incision to receive the sap and to conduct it into troughs underneath. Each family, or firm has its own bush, consisting generally of three or four hundred trees. These are visited in turn by two or more of the younger ladies whose office is to collect the sap and bring it to the fire.

The most experienced among them is placed to regulate the heat, which ought to be tolerably equal, and round her the rest of the party are busied in watching the progress of boiling, and arranging the contents of the kettles, and finally when by steady boiling the consistency of sugar is obtained, in delivering it over to the others, whose business it is to keep stirring the boiling mass as it gradually cools and settles . . ."

The white settler was quick to follow the Indian's lead, and to improve on his methods. Noticing that those trees which had their trunks warmed by the sun gave the most sap, he early began the practice of clearing his sugar bush of underbrush and other unprofitable timber, so letting the sun into it, and at the same time making possible the passage of an ox-drawn sled holding a barrel.

Noting that a tapped tree—a slashed tree—though it gave copiously for a year or two did not thrive thereafter, he put by his tapping hatchet, or tomahawk, and of the Indian method kept only the term. He tapped with an auger, drilling a small hole into which he fitted an alder twig spile, or spigot, in the usual fashion. Later he used spiles made of bent tin, and still later, of cast iron.

Here in Medonte, we make our syrup in the pioneer way still. Though some folk, not too far distant, boast of modern evaporators which turn the sap almost while you watch from pale watery thinness to thick brown syrup, we use the old kettles still, hanging them by logging chains from a heavy timber over a fire-filled pit, and boiling, boiling, and boiling, by dayliight and moonlight, until the job is done.

We say, perhaps making a virtue out of a necessity, that the old way is the best, that pot or kettle syrup is best. We argue that the wood smoke welling up over the boiling sap, curling around the fire-blackened lip of the kettle, gives the syrup a piquancy, a tang that the evaporator syrup lacks. We tell each other, and we believe it, that the bits of charcoal, bark, and wood ash that blow into the boiling sap, to swirl and stew there through all the hours of boiling, give our maple syrup a bouquet, a delicate undertone of flavour that the shielded and coddled product of the evaporator can never hope to attain. However, to-morrow, or the next day, we may own an evaporator . . . Who knows how we shall argue then?

Having no woodlot of our own, Lucy and I worked with our neighbours, wading through the melting snow, drilling neat round holes in the cool rough trunk of every maple tree we could find. The hard maple was our first choice as it gives the sweeter sap, but the soft maple was not neglected for its sap also makes good syrup.

We drilled our tap holes on the south side of the trees, even as the Indians did before us, for like them, we had learned that not only does the sap run best on the sun-warmed side of the trunk, but it runs earlier here and makes better syrup. Farmer Tom followed us, driving spiles into the holes we had drilled, and John, his father, followed him, hanging sap pails to the already dripping spouts.

While the pails filled, all hands busied themselves about the fireplace. The great beach limb, seven inches through and twenty feet long, that was to hold the kettle, was settled even more firmly into its bed on the two heavy timber butts that supported it at either end. The fire-pit beneath was deepened a bit and the stones that walled its sides were built up a tier or two. The huge kettles were hung by logging chains from the beach limb, the fires were lit, and the first sap of the year poured into the caldrons.

Hour after hour, all through the day and most of the night, the fire under the pots was kept blazing. Hour after hour all day long, the patient horses drew a jumper sleigh and a barrel down the bush trails from tree to tree collecting the sap from the brimming pails. Hour after hour we fed the kettles, pouring in sap and still more sap as the boiling diminished that which was already in the pots. The pile of old rails, rotten fence posts, and worm-eaten logwood that was our fuel shrunk alarmingly. We were not much surprised when we were told that it takes a pile of wood eight feet long by four feet wide and four feet high to boil 250 gallons of sap into five gallons of syrup, and that it takes another pile of wood half as big to turn that syrup into hard brown maple sugar.

It seemed that our hours of fire tending would never end, and yet end they did. We were smoke-smudged and blistered, sticky and tired, when at long last John pronounced, quite solemnly, his verdict as kettle boss, that the sap had become syrup, and good syrup at that. Lucy and I looked unbelievingly at the mess in the kettles. Bits of charred wood, charcoal, old leaves and wood ash floated there in the midst of an uninviting looking white scum. It looked like poor porridge, a pig's breakfast to us, and if I remember correctly, we said so.

We were to eat our words. A few hours later, after the syrup had been strained through several thicknesses of clean white muslin, it was carried down to the farm house and set in smaller kettles on the back of the kitchen stove. There it was brought to the boil again and skimmed again. It was skimmed and re-skimmed a dozen times, and cleared to a golden translucency.

We have a trick here in Medonte, a trick that is older than Canada, and which is yet to be improved on. We take fresh eggs, farm fresh eggs, beat them into a bit of cold syrup, and pour the whole into the syrup kettles that we have let cool a bit on the back of the stove. We then stir up the fire, put the kettles over it and watch them come to a boil again. As the syrup reaches the boiling point there is a great heaving and bubbling in the pot, and up from the bottom, in a gray swirling cloud, come the beaten-up eggs, gathering on the way every last little impurity or speck in the syrup. The wooden skimming ladle goes to work again, and a weird mixture of eggs, chips, ash and charcoal is lifted from the surface of the steaming syrup. All that is left behind is clear, golden-brown goodness, the essential sweetness of the micktan tree, the stuff the redman believed to be the blood of the Manitou, the great god of the forest.

# 17

*We Buy Wild Geese*

WITH BLOODROOT BLOOMING BY THE RAIL FENCE AND WITH the shadow of the old log house that is the Owl Pen falling on the scurrying whiteness of our surviving Chanticler chicks, it seemed inevitable that anything added to such a purely Canadian scene should be Canadian too. Our farmer neighbours were not at all surprised when, rising like a trumpet call out of our cross-creek meadow, drowning the loud spring burble of Moonstone Creek, there came one day the weird barbaric "honk-a-honk-a" of the wild grey Canada goose.

"Got a Canadian honker," observed a neighbour.

"Yes," we confessed.

"Suits yer place, somehow." He spat tobacco juice at a roadside violet, missed, and grinned. "Any people that live in a timber house back of rail fences in this day and age would be just plain lost with ordinary sensible barnyard geese, I guess." He went on down the road.

The savage goose cry rose again from our cross-creek meadow. It did fit. It fitted our Medonte hills, and the cedars by the creek. It fitted the elms on the hilltops, and the old stone walls running up to them. It fitted the pine trees, and the crusty independence and forthrightness of our neighbour. Somehow the wild cry of our geese seemed a natural and inevitable part of our Medonte spring song —as though it had always been.

It was not without difficulty that Lucy and I added this bit of Canada to our growing population at Owl Pen, and though we were to be months learning it, our difficulties were not ended. They began with the Doctor, as we called the great horned owl that we kept for a time captive in a wooden box in Lucy's studio. He, like our neighbour, had his bit to say about our Canada geese. He said it to us and to them, and he kept on saying it until we turned his cage face to the wall and so put an end to his chatter.

Our geese arrived without warning, in a wooden crate, and Lucy and I having no pen prepared for them, decided to put them in the studio while we made a place for them in the unkempt little meadow on the far side of the Moonstone. As we carried them, box and all, into the studio, the Doctor, who had been busy with a beef bone, swivelled his great head slowly towards us. He stared moodily, and then as he caught sight of the caged geese, froze into utter stillness. His huge eyes dilated. Their golden yellow burned with an amber flame. Slowly his broad wings lifted. His feathers fluffed. He filled his box. He grew, it seemed, to twice his normal size, and then froze again, a threatening glowering embodiment of envenomed hate that made no move or sound.

At first our geese did not realize that they had other feathered company in this strange new world into which we had carried them. For a moment they were busied recovering their composure after the shaking they had received on their journey. They stared out of their slatted cage at the strange furniture that surrounded them, at the modelling stands, and clay tubs, the curious bits and pieces that are the paraphernalia of the sculptor's art.

It was the goose that first noticed the glowering yellow eyes so banefully fixed on her and her mate. She hissed softly and every jetty feather on her glistening neck rose in a quivering ruff. The gander, his attention thus drawn to the silent threat in the adjoining cage, added his long rasping hiss to hers. The two geese then stood like carven images of geese, regarding a carven owl.

For a long two minutes there was utter silence in the Owl Pen studio. A malignant electric tension filled the air. The geese stared unblinkingly with iron-black specks of eyes. The owl, as was his wont when disturbed, began to stink abominably. Wild and bloody murder was the one thought in the hard bird-minds of all three. Suddenly, as Lucy stirred uneasily, the tension broke. A turbulent gasped "honk-a-honk-a" ripped out of the gaping beaks of the galvanized geese. With long wings spread they rushed the bars of their cage, their mouths wide open and death in their eyes. A thin screamed "sk-r-r-r" came from the owl. He leaped from his perch, flatling against the wooden bars of his cage so that it shook and swayed on its stand. His huge curved talons sank socket deep into the wood. He beat his wings, spat, and screamed again.

"Sk-r-r-r!"

"Honk-a-honk-a!"

The thin frightened wail of a baby kitten cowering under a nearby table was lost in the din. We could see his little mouth opening frantically, but could not hear the sounds that came from it. As we watched, the little fellow gathered all his courage into one small bundle and bolted past the owl's cage for the still open door. He stood not upon the order of his going.

The last thing in the world that Lucy and I wanted to happen was happening. Our geese, nervous and timid creatures at the best of times, had been excited and frightened by their long train and truck journey, worried enough perhaps, to put the goose off her lay and so cost us a breeding year. Now the Doctor was adding his pennyworth to the situation, as though to make sure that the Owl Pen would be without goslings for a twelvemonth at least. I grabbed his cage and spun it, turning its open face to the wall. I thrust a handful of red meat in to him, and still he screamed and cursed us—us and our long-necked geese. In a last desperate effort to quiet him, I flung a couple of feed sacks over his cage turning his day into night.

"Sk-r-r-r!" he screamed again, and was silent.

With peace come again to the Owl Pen, Lucy and I knelt on the studio floor peering in through the heavy slats of the goose cage at the beauties that had come to us out of the Ontario North. Even in the crowded dingy confines of the box, they were magnificent. Though born in a barnyard, they were true scions still of proud wild ancestors who had known the unfettered freedom of the polar wastes. There was wildness still in their beady black eyes which shone with the light of battle. The long proud arch of their jetty necks, their stately carriage, and the steady curve of their lithesome bodies, sang a song, not of barnyard lushness, but of cold clear northern skies. It seemed to us as we knelt there studying them, that some day a prouder nation than this Canada of ours might draw one flying on an oblong of white bunting, and feel that she had a flag behind which her sons could march. We fed them, and said goodnight.

The next morning, with dawn still a thin red stain on the eastern horizon, Lucy and I went out with wire, hammers, and wire cutters, to partition off a corner of our cross-creek pasture as a private park for Lode Star and Wind Wrack, as we had decided to call our stately guests. We hadn't the faintest idea how high a fence it would take to hold them. We did know that the only posts and wire we had available would limit our fence to a mere three feet in height. We looked at our wee roll of wire and then at our hemisphere-hurdling geese, and decided to go ahead with our building. We had not the heart to keep them in their miserable packing box prison for even one day more.

All day long we worked at our fence building, our park making. We dug post holes, strung wire and stretched wire. We nailed wire and tied wire. We bashed our fingers, scratched our legs, and lost our tempers, but as the long sun of evening slanted down over our western borders, we had the satisfaction of seeing Lode Star and Wind Wrack step deliberately out of their box on to the wind-flattened grass of the enclosure.

"Lay nice big eggs," said Lucy to Wind Wrack the goose.

"Do your stuff," said I to Lode Star the gander.

"Honk!" said the gander.

"Skuk!" said the goose.

And they turned their gray backs on us and strode haughtily away.

# 18

## *We Praise Manure*

CLOUD SHADOWS CHASED THEMSELVES OVER THE PLOUGHED
lands of Medonte, across leaning rail fences and fence
corners where gray fingers of snow still lingered, across the
side-road, past the dead hemlock tree and up the far hillside to where the green wheat on the back field of North
Rising Farm thanked the sun. It was farming weather—
farmer's weather—and the whole countryside was filled
with the glory of it—a glory that could be heard as well
as seen.

First of all there was the wind soughing through the
bud-filled tops of the elm trees, laughing and licking at
the apple-green eaves of Owl Pen, and scrawling twisty,
changing pictures on the brown face of Owl Pen pond.
It was a playful wind, an urchin wind, as frolicsome as
springtime and heady with perfume. It ruffled the backs
of our Canada geese, and fluffed the feathers of our white
Chanticler chicks, changing them into little unwilling sloops
and yawls afloat on a sea of grass.

Mixed with the wind sounds and the honk-a-honk of
our geese and the cheeped protests of our chicks was the
blood-stirring caw of distant crows, the faint skr-e-e-e of
a high flying hawk, the pleading of zooming killdeer, and
the comfortable pipe of early robins. There was also to be
heard, as an inevitable undertone to our Medonte spring
song, the raucous roaring of a neighbour whose horses
would not, or could not, draw to suit him, and the uphill
clatter of Farmer Jim's manure-spreader as he drove it
over the stubbles and old furrows of Plum Tree Farm.

To the true countryman, to farm folk with an honest love of good land in their hearts, the iron song of the manure-spreader has more of spring in it, more of spring song in it, than was ever dreamed of in all the bird song and wind song April has ever known. The green-faced gods of country living have seen to it that every faithful worshipper of theirs shall see in its great dirty wheels, as they roll over the flower stems, a finer beauty than the poet sees in lamb-like clouds above a wheat-green hill.

There is a good reason why this should be. Without the manure-spreader and its fragrant load, there would be no wheat-green hill. There might be a dust storm and a hummock in a dust bowl. There might be a desert. There would be no fine checker board of many coloured fields spread over the countryside like a pied piper's cloak. There would be no crooked rail fences, no sprawling stump fences, no old stone walls to stand mnemonic of the generations of calloused hands that have worked to transform the wilderness of the Indians into the rich Medonte farmlands of today.

It is a queer thought, but a demonstrably true one, that except for the reeking manure-spreader there would be no silvery old barns nestling down among gnarled maples beside quiet farm houses or gurgling creeks. Medonte would still be, or would be on the way to becoming again, a land of savage huntsmen. And our cities, denied the endless bounty of our fields, would starve and crumble. Famine and disease would sweep them. Nature has her own pitiless way of dealing with people who grow proud of their machines and indifferent to their soil, and in their own minds superior to the mound by the stable door.

Here in Medonte we suffer from no such delusions of grandeur. When we dip into a big dish of strawberries and cream we know what to thank for its goodness. When we see pictures in the magazines of a grand lady seated

on a carved chair and reaching with a silver spoon into a
china bowl, we know that for all the garniture, she sits on a
tree stump and reaches into a manure pile. Having no veil
of unreality spread between us and the soil we all live by, we
see nothing distasteful in such a picture. As a matter of
fact, we find it beautiful, in the deeper meaning of the
word.

So up the hill went Lucy and I to watch Farmer Jim
get rid of the great pile of manure piled against the back
end of his barn. Down the narrow lane, shadowed by the
wild plum trees that give his farm its name, he drove the
lumbering spreader. If there was a thought in his mind,
it was to remember to dodge the low-hanging branch of
the ancient apple tree at the bend, a branch heavy enough
and low enough to sweep a man from such a lofty perch
as his. If there was a light in his eyes, it was born of the
thought that he was, after a long winter, getting on the
land again, doing the springtime chore that has been part
of every spring he could remember, a chore that his father
did before him, a chore that his son, or somebody else's
son, will be doing when he is gone.

"It's giving back what has been taken," he said. "It's
paying a debt to the land."

As the back-end of the manure-spreader passed through
the fence gap into the big back field, Jim moved the gear
handle of the machine forward, and with an appreciative
glance at the great tines that whirred and clacked into
life, watched the golden treasure of his barnyard, the precious by-product of his winter husbandry, spatter out over
the hungry ground. It was easy to see from the expression
on Jim's face that the sight was to him a good one.

Down the long field lurched the heavy machine, the
big tines whirling, the manure flying, the horses nodding
at the sun. Birds rose in panic from the pelted hedge rows.
Jack-rabbits raced wildly for the shelter of the nearby

woods. Chipmunks in the stone piles scolded and chattered at this invasion of their kingdom. Jim, too intent on the even spreading of his load to notice half the tumult his work occasioned, drove blissfully on, around and around the field until his spreader was empty.

When at last the field was finished and the last load spread, when all the young spring growth in it was blackened and flattened under a carpet of rotten straw, Farmer Jim put the bars back in the fence gap, and paused to consider and judge his morning's work. He saw honest country beauty in the well-spread field. He noted, with a grin, a timid jack-rabbit loping back to its nest in the hedgerow. His nose wrinkled appreciatively as the wind veered and brought the rich smell of the field to him. He lit his pipe, and squinted his eyes a bit.

I think Jim, in his mind's eye, was seeing the ploughing to be done in a few days' time. Leaning there on a fence rail split by his pioneer forefathers, he was seeing the littered field change at his plough-point into a bare expanse of carefully drawn furrows. He was seeing the disking and harrowing that was to be done to make a good seed bed. He was seeing the red seed drill, the slowly pacing horses, and the cloud of grey dust over them. He was seeing the field, left to the rains and warm sun, stirring almost visibly with new and eager life as the small seeds sprouted and reached upwards through the soil to the sun, feeding endlessly, eagerly, on the richness he had spread.

Lucy and I, as we stood there beside him, were yet far ahead of him in our imagining. We were already, in our minds, seeing the harvest home. We were seeing the oats, or barley, whichever might be, falling in a whispering golden cascade before the clacking binder. We were seeing the sheaves piled into fat stooks, tossed onto rumbling wagons, carried into the dim cathedral vastness of the barn. All this we could see standing in a cold spring wind looking at a brown field that was littered with manure.

There was a time when Lucy and I would have seen much less. There was a time when we would have seen only scenery, and spoiled scenery at that. Over our heads like a tent would have gone the fact that rural loveliness is the unconsidered by-product of rural labour, that farm-land beauty is born of rural blood and sweat, and brown manure.

# PART 7

## Dreams Are Fish

*I love at early morn, from new mown swath,*
*To see the startled frog his route pursue;*
*To mark while leaping o'er the dripping path,*
*His bright sides scatter dew . . .*

JOHN CLARE, 1864

# 19

*We Go Fishing*

IT MAY BE THAT WE SHOULD HAVE KEPT OUR NOSES TO THE grindstone, so to speak, and kept on with our gardening, our building, and our chicken-tending, but the spade kept turning up fishworms, the perches we were putting into our new range shelters looked so much like fishing poles, and the litter fork kept looking like nothing on earth so much as an oversized fish spear. We tried hard to be practical, but the running waters of Moonstone Creek kept burbling in our ears. Somehow—it just happened—we found ourselves walking away from the Owl Pen towards the pool below the dam. With the work piling up, it was, in the words of a neighbour, "just plain aggravatin' ".

But how can a man be expected to keep his mind and his hand to the daily task, when he lives in the springtime in a country that nature has wrinkled into a thousand little hills? How can a woman be expected to concentrate on chickens, even white Canadian Chanticler chickens, when she knows that at the foot of every hill is a little stream where cresses and trilliums grow? How can either man or woman be expected to keep to their garden close when they know that in every one of those little streams are crimson-spotted trout, small chub, and most disconcertingly of all in the springtime of the year, great silver-sided sucker fish with purse-like mouths and an inherited inability to dodge a three-pronged spear? Lucy and I followed the bubbles out of the waterfall down the tree-shadowed stream.

We walked down the side of the creek along a path that was rutted inches deep in the spongy turf. It was, quite probably, a cow path made by generations of wandering cattle during the hundred odd years that the valley has been farmed; but we like to think that it is a path that had been merely deepened by the cattle, a path that had been made in the beginning by Indian fishermen who had carried fish spears, even as we carried them, for hundreds of years before the white man came to Medonte, a path that might well have known the feet of the early Jesuit missionaries in the days when Medonte was part of New France.

Fathers Brebeuf and Lalemant would never recognize the Medonte of to-day, cleared of its great pine forests, cleared of its warring Indians, a smiling land of sunny little farms and quiet villages. They would seek in vain the great towns of the Hurons that once crowned every other hill. They would not know where to look for the tumbled foundation stones of their missions. All that they would recognize as being part of the old blood-spattered Medonte that they knew, would be the silvery sucker fish still lurking in the clear cold pools of Moonstone Creek.

Suckers were an important part of the economy of old

Medonte. The Indians depended on them for their first big spring feast, the ceremonial gorging that ended the hunger moons, the winter months. The Indians feasted on them, grew fat on them, and when they had eaten all they could of them, smoked them, dried them, and put them away in stinking bales against future need. Even in their crude husbandry they found use for the sucker fish, for they buried them, one fish to each hill, with their corn and pumpkin seeds. It was their way, hundreds of years ago, of feeding the land that was in due time to feed them.

With the coming of the white man, the sucker lost none of its importance. It remained still in lakeless Medonte the first of spring bounties after the maple run. The first Canadians went suckering as gleefully as they went sugaring. They fried the fish, baked them, boiled them, roasted them, and pickled them in spiced vinegar. They packed them away by the boiled and salted barrelful in cool cellars, and they spread them by the ton on their fields.

In pioneer times the big fish ran in the creeks in numbers unguessed at to-day. It was not a matter then of seeking a lonely elusive skulker in the shadows of a deeper pool. The creeks, much bigger then than they are now, were literally black with suckers when the run was on. The settlers caught them by throwing a mound of brush across a stream, thus forming a sort of twig net. Having done this they would walk upstream a hundred yards or so, pull off their boots, roll up their pantaloons, and walk back down stream in the centre of the channel driving the fish before them.

Long before they reached the twig obstruction, the creek in front of them would be literally seething with piled-up masses of frightened fish. It was then merely a matter of forking them out with a hay fork or a manure fork, on to the bank or into an ox-drawn wagon or sled drawn up handily at the water's edge.

Lucy and I talked of these things as we walked along the creek side through the deep ravine that cuts across Green Shadows Farm. We walked on until we came to a bend where an old basswood tree leaned over a grassy bank, and there we sat down. The day was warm. The air was still, and filled with the heady fragrance that sunlight strikes in the springtime from mosses and damp turf. We lit cigarettes and lay back. It was nice to just lie there and think, a little guiltily perhaps, of the work we had fled, and of our white Chanticler chicks.

Our chickens, having survived our first bungled beginnings with them, had thrived. They had grown in stature by the hour it seemed, and at three weeks of age were more than three parts feathered. Lucy and I had begun to dream dreams of ourselves, and our chickens, wearing red ribbons at the local fair. We put away the nursery boxes in the kitchen. We gave unasked-for advice to our neighbours. We grew cocky.

Nemesis struck. One after another, a disturbing number of our chicks lost the use of their legs. While they remained bright, perky, vivacious little demons from the knees up, they changed into flabby little corpses from the knees down. Their tiny feet curled under them. They became knock-kneed. They hobbled on their hocks.

Lucy and I went to our books, our ever present help in time of trouble, and turned up those sections which have to do with the ills and ailments of chickdom. Our reading suggested that our chicks were suffering from a fungi disease brought about by mouldy food or litter. Lucy and I agreed, after much argument, on that. We blamed the litter, mixed oat and wheat straw which we had bought from a town dealer.

Out to the brooder house we went and examined it. The straw looked all right. It felt all right. It smelled all right. We applied the only remaining test we could think of. We ate some, and it tasted like any other straw to us, perhaps even a little more so, for the chicks had been sleeping in it for a week. We ate a little more, just to be sure. It still tasted all right, and we continued to feel all right. We ruled out the straw as the cause of our troubles and went back to our books. We read for an hour, and shrugged hopelessly. Our chicks had symptoms to fit every disease in the books.

"Eeny, meeny, miney, mo," sighed Lucy.

"Perhaps it's just a passing sort of thing," I hazarded.

"Perhaps," said Lucy.

We decided to do nothing for a while and see what happened. The days went by, and we put our infirmary boxes back under the kitchen stove. We filled them to overflowing. We got more boxes. Chicks died. With five expensive range shelters under construction in our pasture field and with a forty-eight foot laying house about to be begun, we were faced with the prospect of having nothing to put in them when they were completed. Every trip to the brooder house saw at least one more cripple brought back to the kitchen infirmary. The smoke of burning corpses mingled with the wood smoke in the kitchen chimney.

In a wild panic, we telephoned the local veterinary. He listened for a while to our gushed and tangled tale of woe, to our list of carefully noted symptoms, and then grunted his diagnosis. Our chickens were suffering from a vitamin deficiency.

"Impossible," we argued, and read him the label from one of our feed bags, a label that guaranteed that the mash we were feeding our chicks contained everything that even the most pampered of little chicks might need, everything from soup to nuts.

"Maybe you ought to read that label to your chicks," snorted the vet. "They might believe it; I don't. You can believe me when I tell you that your birds are suffering from a vitamin deficiency, and that they need milk, raw milk or sweet milk, milk powder or buttermilk. Good-day!"

We telephoned our feed merchant, and he, after expressing polite unbelief, succumbed like ourselves to the weight of evidence and professional opinion, and sent us a twenty pound bag of milk powder. It was a drop in the bucket of our need. We telephoned our cow-keeping neighbours. Contributions flowed in. Our kitchen and our brooder house, and our chickens, literally swam in milk, sour milk, sweet milk, buttermilk, and powdered milk. Our chicks drank greedily. In three days they were all walking again, and Lucy and I breathed easily again.

At last the day arrived when it was time to take our chicks, fine big chicks with fine white feathers, bright eyes, and golden legs, out of the brooder house nursery of their babyhood, and put them into the range shelters that were to be their home until they were fully grown. The transfer would have been easy if our books had not insisted that our birds would grow faster and be happier, if the sexes were segregated. It didn't seem logical to us, but who were we, mere beginners in poultry husbandry, to question authority?

Anyone passing the Owl Pen that day must have been been quite sure that we were stark staring mad. Our bad-tempered shouting could be heard at least as far as our neighbour's barn as we argued the sex of our adolescent chickens.

"It's a cockerel!"

"It's a pullet!"

"Damn it all, any fool can see that . . . "

"It's a pullet!"

It seemed impossible to us that any feathered youngsters who were so much alike as our chicks were, pullets and cockerels, could have any bad effect on each other. Maybe they differed in their mental attitude, or in their spiritual development. Physically, they seemed as much alike, where it mattered most, as peas in a pod. What they could do to each other beyond a bit of kicking and biting was beyond us. But the books said separate them, so separate them we did, as best we could. The cockerels were a little longer in the leg, we decided. The pullets were a little redder in the face. The cockerels were more upright in their carriage. The pullets had longer tails. It was nonsensical.

At last we finished. As a committe of two for the suppression of vice, or just plain healthy funning, Lucy and I had done our best. Our pullets were locked in two shelters on the east end of the range. The cockerels were shut into two more shelters that we had crowded to the west side of our field. As advised by our reading, we kept them locked in for a full twenty-four hours.

According to our books, pullets and cockerels would, after such confinement, always return to their own shelters. When the recommended interval had elapsed, we let them out. We opened the shelter doors and watched our white wonders fly, peeping with delight, out of their pretty red-roofed shelters, to the fresh young grass. That night we found them all, piled three and four deep, on the sagging floor and perches of one small bulging shelter.

With a shrug of resignation, we began the silly job all over again, working in lamp-lit darkness this time, thrusting squawking pullets into this cardboard box, thrusting squeaking cockerels into that cardboard box, lugging the filled boxes through a drizzling rain to this shelter and that shelter, so many into this one, so many into that. We banged our knees, and bumped our heads, and skinned our shins. We hated our chickens that night, and our chickens, I am sure, hated us. We hated them, and yet, as they shuddered away from us in the darkness of the shelters, we pitied them for the distress we were so obviously causing them.

There was no point in trying to explain to them that what we did, we did for their own good, that they would not grow up to be big cocks and stout hens if virtue and virginity were not inflicted upon them during the months of their youth. Thank heavens we didn't even try to explain! We might even have spared them our pity, for the next night they were all back together again, in one bulging shelter again, crowded together again, piled like cordwood again, squawking with discomfort, and panting for breath. We sorted them out again. The following night we sorted them a fourth time.

What fatal fascination that one range shelter had for our chicks, we will never know. What they had against our other three shelters, we cannot guess. Only one thing was clear, and that was that the nightly struggle was doing neither ourselves, nor our chicks, any good. We gave it up, deciding that if our birds had not the decency to keep to their own dormitories, they could take the consequences, whatever they might be. We told them so. The precocious brats clucked their amusement. The days passed, and the weeks passed, and they grew like weeds.

"The sinful shall flourish for a time," quoted Lucy.

"That's all we ask," said I.

It was good, lying under the trees. We thought of the fishing we had come to do, and fingered our spears, but somehow thinking of fish made us think of our cat, Titch. Or maybe it was the chickens that brought her to mind. Titch had come to the Owl Pen because she was a chicken killer. She had come to die. Her previous owner had found it impossible to break her of a fatal liking for chicken meat, live chicken meat. For months Titch had stalked and killed chicks in the fields about Four Winds Cottage. When she had practically wiped out the home flock, she had carried her hunting abroad into neighbouring barnyards.

"Please take her," pleaded her owner, "my children would never forgive me if I . . . if I . . . if I . . . "

We took her. We were to keep her just long enough to allow the memory of her to fade in the minds of the two little girls at Four Winds who idolized her. Then we were to destroy her, or have her destroyed. We didn't. We couldn't. She was such an affectionate little cat.

Our chicks arrived. Titch stood entranced in the shadow of the brooder house, listening to their peeping. We shook our heads. Invalids found their way into the cardboard infirmary by the kitchen stove. We filled a saucer with milk and set it by the chick-filled box. A test had to be made. A lesson had to be learned. It it wasn't . . . Well, if it wasn't . . . We hardened our hearts.

Titch came at our call, rubbed her head against our legs, and went to her saucer. With her head half-way to the milk she suddenly froze. A chick had peeped. Very slowly her head lifted. Her ears went back. Her eyes dilated. She put her paws on the edge of the box, lifted herself up, and looked in. Her tail twitched. She looked at the chicks huddled below her. Her jaws trembled. She looked up at us, then dropped to the floor again and fled, pell-mell, from the kitchen. Though we did our best to coax her back, she would not come. She did without her milk until we brought it to her, out of the kitchen into the dining room. We fed her pure cream that night.

Titch never did touch a chick of ours. As the days passed, she continued to ignore them with almost comical determination. She either could not, or would not, abide their presence. If we wanted to see the last of her for hours, all we had to do was take an ailing chick out of the box in the kitchen and offer it to her. Titch's ears would go straight back and she would flee the room, and the house too, if the door happened to be open.

"Queer," murmured Lucy drowsily.

"Queer," said I.

We snuggled down among the dry leaves on the creek

bank. The silence filled with the spring-song of a hundred unseen birds. The tree branches blurred, changed slowly into a wavering criss-cross of beckoning Indian arms, white chickens, Jesuit robes, ancient fishing spears, and cats. Fishing was forgotten. Our cigarettes went out. We slept.

# 20

### We Free a Murderer

LUCY AND I CAME BACK FROM OUR WALK BY MOONSTONE Creek with our spears unwetted, and with no fish to fry. We had enjoyed the day. We had walked among flowers, and talked among trees, and slept in the springtime sun.

"I'm thinking," said Lucy, as we walked from the creek bottom to the concession line, "I'm thinking of the Doctor. I'm thinking of the dirty, old reprobate sitting in his bean box prison in the studio. I'm thinking how miserable he must be, locked up indoors on a day like this. I keep thinking of how he smells. I keep thinking of how he curses us. I keep thinking how beautiful he would look, to a she-owl anyway, flying in the moonlight past that spray of hawthorne blossom by the rail fence."

There was no doubt about it. The time had come, as we had long known it evenutally must, when we had to give our caged owl either the freedom of the hills and woods, his natural heritage, or the kindly oblivion of a quick death, the decency of a bullet between his splendid eyes. The thought of him huddled in all his magnificent savagery and fierce independence among mouldy bones and soiled straw in an old bean box, sorted badly with our own enjoyment of spring by Moonstone Creek.

The mere fact that in keeping him prisoner we had saved his life didn't alter or help the situation a bit. He had been caged long enough, for several months, since early in the winter when a farmer friend brought him to us on the back of his truck.

"I've brought you a visitor," he said.

Lucy and I went around to the back of the truck, and peered into the slatted box that was there. We found ourselves peering into the golden yellow eyes of one of the largest horned owls ever taken in this part of Ontario. It stood nearly two feet high, and had a wing-spread of nearly six feet. Its talons were horrible things, cruelly curved, and strong enough to tear flesh and muscle and sinew from the arm of a man. Its beak was like a two-edged scimitar, designed to slash and rend.

"We found where he had torn the head of a jack-rabbit," said the farmer. "We put a trap beside what was left of it, and when the owl came back for another feed, we got him by one claw. We were going to kill him—maybe we should have—but we thought of you, and the name of your place, and thought you might like him." He thrust his face towards the slatted front of the box, and the great owl jabbed at him, with a lightning thrust of its heavy beak. "Friendly little fellow, always aims for your eyes." He grinned, and set the box down in the snow beside our gate. "Be good to him." He climbed back into his truck, waved, and was gone.

All during the winter, while Lucy and I worked in the studio at our bee equipment, preparing for the spring-time arrival of our honey bees, we had the owl for company. We fed him beef scraps, and offal, and dead chicks from our brooder house and kitchen nursery. We robbed Titch, our cat, of the mice she caught and begged our neighbours for the bodies of whatever mice they managed to trap or kill. School children, on their way to the red brick school house on the side road, took to leaving dead mice, rats, and squirrels in our mail box. Our owl grew fat, but not less wild, and the only thanks we ever got from him was, as time went on, an inclination to ignore us rather than slash at us with beak or claws.

Now we had decided to give him back the freedom of

his native hills. We knew we were being silly. As good countrymen, good chicken farmers, we should have taken him, and a rifle, out to a hole dug among the wild flowers by the creek. We should have told ourselves that we were dealing with one of the worst killers of the woodlands, a wanton murderer whose idea of good fun it is to get into a chicken yard and there, in a matter of minutes, tear the heads from ten, or forty hens. We should have remembered what he did to the jack-rabbit, and what he would do to any little bird or beast that came within reach of his curved beak or mighty claws. We should have put a red hot bullet through his heavy skull.

We didn't. Our Great Horned Owl was too beautiful to kill. He was going free. That was our decision. That night we carried his last prison meal to him, a half-grown cockerel, a cull that had been ailing, and which I had destroyed. The big owl blinked his orange eyes at us as we carried the dead chicken to his cage. He flexed his huge talons so that they sank slowly out of sight in the tattered billet of wood that was his perch. He huffed his feathers, half-spread his wings, opened his cruel beak, and cursed us with a cold intensity that, as usual, made the short hairs rise on our necks.

As we forced the dead chicken through the cage slats, the owl came forward, and with a sudden thrust of his heavy beak, took it from us. He sank his claws effortlessly into its crumpled white breast. He glared his hate at us, cursed us again, and tore off the cockerel's head. He tore off a wing. He snapped a leg in two. Through a mask of bloody white feathers that stuck to his champing beak, he hissed and growled at us. He tore flesh from flesh, and bone from bone, gulped, and cursed some more. He was magnificent, and he was horrible.

The next day a friend came visiting, and we borrowed his car. We loaded the Doctor, cage and all, into the rumble seat. Down the concession line we sped with him, out of Moonstone Valley away from Moonstone Creek. Up over Stone Wall Hill we went, past Four Winds Cottage, on to the Fair Valley side road, and the big bush lot that is there. We took the cage out of the car, set it by the road side, tore off the slats, and stood back. Our Great Horned Owl, our beautiful son of the moonrise, our flying delirium, was free.

The Doctor didn't seem much impressed by this turn of events. He sat quietly on his perch, staring unconcernedly about, showing no eagerness at all to get out of his box. He blinked solemnly at a daisy that nodded nearby, and flexed the talons of one foot idly in what was left of the chicken on his cage floor. The minutes crept by. He still didn't come out. I picked up a stick and moved forward. The big owl stepped out of his box. I thought he was coming to meet me. The skin on my head crinkled. The owl spread his mighty wings. He didn't seem to fly. He seemed literally to drift away, like an over-sized bit of thistle-down, to a nearby pine stump. I took another step in his direction. He drifted again to another stump, and sat there looking back, almost longingly I thought, towards the dirty bean box. For a moment I thought he was going to fly back into it. He didn't.

At that moment there came drifting faintly down wind the distance-softened cawing of a lonely crow. The great horned owl on the tree stump swivelled his head sharply in the direction of the sound, and stood motionless again, except for his blinking eyes. The cawing came again, closer this time. The owl hissed softly. A second crow cawed. Two dim black specks appeared in the eastern sky. Three dim specks. Four dim specks. The sky filled with the cawing of crows, with the flap-flap-flap of frantic wings. Caw-caw! Caw-caw! It was a battle cry. The crows had spotted their ancient enemy.

The owl on the tree stump hissed and stamped, and lifted himself into the air again. It may be that the old fellow, so long denied the use of his wings, found flying a bit of a chore. It could be that his fierce nature relished, after the soul-killing monotony of his bean box existence, a chance to do beak and claw battle with the hereditary enemies of his kind. Whatever the reason may have been, he did not hurry to the protection of the nearby wood. He did not even try to reach its edge. He flew slowly to yet another stump, one backed by scrubby cedar trees, and there settled himself to meet the onslaught of the screaming black cloud of crows that now filled the air above him.

So we left him, chuttering quietly to himself, flexing his talons two inches deep into the rotten wood of his stump top perch, waiting—waiting—waiting. As we drove away we saw the crows zooming downward. We heard wild shrieks. We did not feel sorry for our outnumbered owl. Our sorrow was reserved for the Fair Valley crows.

# 21

## *We Dote on Ducklings*

BABY DUCKLINGS ARE AS SAINTLY AS BABY CHICKS ARE
devilish, and even more lovely to observe. Baby ducks are
adorable little things. I was glad that it was not possible
for us to put our first twenty-five where they should have
been put, in the big brooder house lately vacated by our
mule-headed Chanticler chicks. There, with a thermo-
statically controlled coal stove burning merrily, with a
huge steel hover to act as foster mother, they would have
been quite happy.

But I had cut a large hole in the brooder house roof,
preparatory to fitting an elegant steel ventilator into it,
and the ventilator had not arrived. I had allowed several
thousand feet of lumber to be piled on top of our coal
supply in the storage shed, and had not taken it away.
I had stepped on one of the thermostat wafers, and had not
been able to replace it. The brooder house was out of
the question.

"So is my kitchen," warned Lucy, grim with forebodings
of what was to be. "I've shared my kitchen with cats
and chickens, kittens and owls. Ducks are out!"

There was, I decided, one other way of caring for our
ducklings so soon to arrive. We could put them under
broody hens, if we had broody hens.

"Which we haven't," snorted Lucy. "Think again." She
tapped the living room table with a stiff forefinger. "And
while you're thinking, don't loose sight of the fact that my
kitchen is out. No darned duck nursery there!"

After some further discussion, it was decided that we

should turn to our neighbours for help. We fondly believed that we would have no difficulty at all in parting them, at a price, from a few fat clucking hens, broodies that would take kindly to our broad-billed orphans, and set their pretty webbed feet safely on the way that pretty webbed feet should go. We got barrels from town and set them up as nests. We designed nice little slatted barricades to protect hens and ducklings from night-prowling marauders. Then we went confidently up the hill to Plum Tree Farm.

"Sorry," said Alice. "We'll need every broody we can get for our own baby chicks."

We went, a little less confidently, to Old Inn Farm. "Sorry," said the mistress of the house, "I've just put eggs under all my broodies."

We went with no confidence at all to Green Shadows Farm.

"We don't keep hens," said the farmer's wife.

I turned hopelessly to Lucy, and Lucy sighed. "I know —my kitchen." She threw up her hands. "Bring on your ducks."

Our ducklings arrived the next afternoon, and we were, in our own way, ready to receive them. We had placed a pair of boxes, lately filled with bee equipment, beside the kitchen stove, and lined them with clean newspapers. In the centre of each box, perched grandly on a china saucer, and shining like the sun, was our own home-made version of a mechanized duck mother. We had taken two empty tomato cans, punched small holes in the sides of them, fitted them with an electric light bulb each, inverted them into a pair of slightly larger coffee tins, and set them on the saucers. I was proud of my invention.

"We'll have either roast duck or a house fire," said Lucy dubiously.

Opening our carton of ducklings was like opening the

bronze lid of an old chest on a jumble of antique jewelry. Our ducklings were jewels indeed. Some of them were tawny yellow and dusty black. Others were like new gold, and still others were like shining bits of silver filigree. Their wee orange beaks were bright and translucent, like flakes of coloured wax, or thin, dyed ivory. Their fragile legs, and ridiculously small webbed feet, were like little crooked branches of rare coral. They didn't quack. They peeped, like so many silver whistles. And yet, for all their beauty, they were pathetically like little lost clowns as they pattered, stumbled, and swayed about in their travel-stained cardboard box.

Having read, to our amazement, that baby ducklings, like baby chicks, have to be taught to drink, we proceeded solemnly with this chore. Carefully, ever so carefully, we picked them up, one at a time, and dunked their pretty little bills into a cup of warm water. Carefully, ever so carefully, for we could not get over the fear that the delicate wee mites might come apart in our hands, we put them down in their new homes, and watched them cuddle up to their 40 watt incandescent mothers.

It was fun teaching the little blighters to drink. After a first moment of surprise and investigation, they gulped, and gurgled, and twisted with delight in our hands. When, a little while later, we put fountains of water on the new spring floors of their new homes, they rolled and wallowed, and cavorted in them. They spooned up the water in their tiny beaks, sprayed it out of their nostrils, spurted it over their backs. They stood knee-deep in their drinking water, twitching with rapture, and they drank it only after they had completely exhausted the first fine frenzy of sitting in it.

Watching them at their fun, it was hard for us to believe our books when they told us that the one thing likely to kill a baby duckling was too much water, especially cold water. A walk in long grass, dampened by a heavy dew, can be fatal to ducklings, our books told us. Exposure to a sudden shower is almost certain to cause death, and one might as well beat them with an axe handle as let them swim before they are six weeks old, said our duck books. We filled the water fountains again and put dishes full of food beside them.

The second act of our farmland comedy was on. Our little jewels, jewels no longer, waded into their food like little pigs, and like bedraggled little pigs at that. They moved with speed. They were like waddling lightning bolts. They grabbed a billful of mash, and then worked their tiny heads like little riveting machines, back and forth in a blue blurr of motion, literally jerking the food back into their gullets, and so down into their pendulous wee crops. A gulp of food, a gulp of water, a hundred jerks . . . that was the order of their meal-time. They had no manners at all.

When all the food was gone, and we had taken away the empty dishes, and the water fountains, they stood about in little groups on the water-soaked newsprint yelling frantically for more, more, more! When it was not forthcoming, they fell to preening themselves, showing us a fastidiousness unguessed at by any other bird, and by few human beings. They missed no single wisp of down on any part of their bodies. One moment they were untidy little bundles of mash and water-smeared fluff. The next moment they were again immaculate little jewels, and Lucy and I found ourselves thinking of them again, not as little web-footed pigs, but as lovely, old-fashioned brooches come somehow to life.

It seemed a shame to us that ducklings should ever grow up to be ducks.

# PART 8

## Of Bees and Ducks

*I think I could turn and live with animals, they are so
    placid and self-contained;*
*I stand and look at them long and long.*
*They do not sweat and whine about their condition;*
*They do not lie awake in the dark and weep for their
    sins . . .*

WALT WHITMAN, 1892

# 22

## *We Establish a Bee-yard*

THE EVENING BEGAN QUIETLY ENOUGH. FROGS FILLED THE twilight with their sweet mating song. Robins chittered to sleep in the brooding cedar trees. Lucy and I sat together on the bank of Moonstone Creek, talking in undertones, tossing little twigs into the swirling water for the trout to jump at them. Peace was everywhere, in the air above us, in the water in front of us, in the grass and flowers beside us, but peace was not in us. Lucy and I were waiting hopelessly, patiently, for the arrival of our bees, which were speeding towards us by truck on the last lap of their long journey from the southern United States.

We were, we told ourselves over and over again, ready for their arrival. Fifty white beehives, the fine fruit of our winter's labour, stood in prim lines on the level greens-

ward in the valley behind us. We had set them out by
chalk line, measuring rod, and spirit level. Each white hive
stood squarely on a black hive-stand, with a dainty alighting board painted either pale blue, grey, green, or pink,
in front of it. Each hive was fitted with the required number of frames, and each frame carried a full sheet of beeswax, which the bees would draw out into honeycomb and
fill with honey—we hoped.

It was not that we had done that which we ought not
to have done, or even that we had left undone that which
we ought to have done. Our preparations had been thor-
ough. Nothing had been overlooked. My new bee gloves
and bee veil lay handily beside my new hive tools, and
new hive smoker, on top of one of the new hives. Our
outward quietude, our inner tumult was occasioned simply
by the fact that we knew absolutely nothing about bees,
nothing except what we had read. I had never seen a
queen bee. Lucy had never been stung.

We had been advised to start our bee keeping modestly,
with one or two hives at most, and so get to know something about their little occupants, before even thinking of
establishing a bee-yard of commercial proportions. We
had disregarded this good advice. We were starting with
fifty hives. Fifty three-pound packages of bees, a total of
some 750,000 bees, honey bees, stinging bees, were speeding towards us, would soon be with us. All that we had
to do when they arrived was tear the tops off the fifty
packages, and tuck the barbed and angry hordes that were
in them safely away in the dark interiors of our fifty pretty
white hives.

Such a chore, we knew, would be a mere nothing, child-
play indeed, to an experienced bee-master, a veteran of
many bee-yard seasons. But we weren't veterans. This
was to be our first season. We were in no position to mini-
mize the horrific experience so soon to be ours. When our

bee packages arrived, we would have to take our bees out of their cages. We would have to handle them. We would have to sit among them. We would have to put them to bed, tuck them in, as it were, feed them, and soothe them. We remembered reading of people, expert bee people, being stung to death. We hoped that our bee gloves would be thick enough, that our bee veils would fit tightly enough, that our overalls would prove sufficient armour to save us from such a fate.

"I think I remember reading somewhere that bees won't sting a person who has washed with carbolic soap," I told Lucy.

"I have some carbolic soap in the house," she whispered.

"I think we have time," I quavered.

We went into the house, and we both took a bath. We lathered ourselves from head to foot with pink carbolic soap. We let the wind dry us, and we left the lather on.

"I feel awful," said Lucy, "and I smell worse."

Like condemned felons watching the approach of their executioner, we watched the bee truck roll into the Owl Pen work yard. We swallowed our hearts, adjusted veils and gloves, and went down to meet it. The Owl Pen bee-yard was about to be established. We wondered if we would live to enjoy it.

As we approached the truck we became aware of a mighty buzzing, a tremendous, murmuring hum. It could have been a million telephone wires humming in a whirlwind. We knew it wasn't. We knew that it was our bees that we heard. We went around to the back of the truck and stared at them piled in a great howling mound of wire screened boxes. With open mouths and bulging eyes, we heard the driver telling us, in a voice that sounded dim and far off, that the bees had travelled well, that few of them were dead, and that all of them were vigorous.

I thought he said "vicious",

"Vigorous," he corrected.

"Oh," I moaned, thankfully.

It would not have been so bad if the bees had arrived in the early hours of the morning, or, for that matter, at any time during the day. Then we would have been able to go about our unaccustomed task in the blessed light of day, and being able to see and study our little charges, we might have gathered a little confidence in our ability to deal with them. But no such luck was ours. Our bees arrived just at dark, with a new moon riding over them, and with them arrived word that they had been a long time in their packages and should be released immediately. Lucy and I lit lanterns, took a long last look at the Owl Pen, said good-bye to the truck driver, and opened the first of the packages.

The next few hours were like a dream—a bad dream. I knelt in the tree-shrouded darkness of the valley with the package full of bees between my knees. Lucy held the lantern. I pulled out the feeder can that hung under the box top, and saw that at least two thousand bees were clinging to it. Goose pimples, as big as pineapples, rose all over me. Lucy made a thin, shuddery, whistling sound as she breathed. I drew out the little cage, in which the queen along with her court of worker bees was imprisoned, and saw that it, too, was covered with a flowering mass of angry bees. I felt myself growing old. I looked up at Lucy. She looked less like a woman than a graven statue of a woman, a graven image of horror. She tried to smile. She couldn't. I tried to smile. My lips felt like wire.

Carefully, ever so carefully, I did as I had been instructed to do by the dealer who had provided our bees. I drew out the cork that closed the queen cage, and then placed it between two of the five comb-carrying frames with which the hive was fitted. Then, drawing a deep breath, I picked up the roaring package, and holding it between my gloved hands, shook out the 15,000 outraged and furious insects that filled it. They rained down into the hive. They fell in great, soft, crawling masses into the vacant space reserved for them, and which was later to be filled with more comb-carrying frames. They rained down, and they crawled up. They welled up over the sides of the hive, and overflowed it. They filled the air. They covered my gloves. They crawled in buzzing hundreds over my overalls. They darkened my veil. I was sure they were getting into my veil. At that moment I didn't like bees very much.

We put the lid back on the hive. That was one package disposed of. We had only forty-nine more to do. We moved to the next hive, to the next package. The roar in the bee-yard grew louder. Six angry bees buzzed inside my veil. They buzzed like a million. I was sure they were a million. They all sat down on me. They stung like scorpions. I felt my left ear swelling. I felt my right ear swelling. I felt my neck swelling. I felt like a pin cushion. I crushed two more of the blighters as they crawled up my legs, inside my trousers. I remembered a tale told me by an old bee-keeper friend.

"I got stung once where no man ought ever to get stung. Wh-o-o-o! H-o-o-o! Don't ever let that happen to you. H-o-o-o! H-o-o! Wear bicycle clips!"

I didn't have any bicycle clips. While I worried over this, several more bees found their way into my gloves. My hands began to swell. The gloves had been too big. Soon they felt too small. I took them off. My hands were like footballs.

"There's a bee inside my veil," moaned Lucy.

While I looked for it, more bees got inside my trousers, I don't know what their target was. I killed them about knee level. There were no bees in Lucy's veil. She wouldn't believe me. While we argued the point, two more got inside my veil and stung me again on the neck. My neck changed into a cross between a summer-sausage and a slab of rising bread dough. We took time off for tea.

I don't know to this day how long an experienced bee-keeper, working by lantern light, and without bicycle clips, would take to hive fifty packages of bees. I do know that working as fast as we dared, it took Lucy and me from 8.30 at night to 3.30 in the morning. I don't know how tired a veteran of the bee-yard would be when he had finished such a chore. I do know that when we finished, we staggered into the Owl Pen, too tired even to think of climbing the stairs to bed.

We collapsed into chairs in front of the cold fireplace, and stared at it blankly. My whole body seemed on fire from the bee poison that had been injected into it. Lucy, fortunately unstung, was white and drawn. Somehow we both managed a smile. The job was done. The Owl Pen bee-yard, a dream for years, was at last a reality. The clock ticked another half hour by.

We went to bed.

# 23

## *We Suspect a Scandal*

OUR DUCKLINGS GREW LIKE SCANDAL ON A CONCESSION line. They lost their jewel-like colour and fragility. Their legs thickened. Their tiny, wax-like bills grew broad and heavy. They doubled in size within a week of their arrival, and overflowed their nursery boxes by the kitchen stove. We provided larger boxes. They overflowed them. They yammered constantly for food, and Lucy mixed her bread, and did her cooking in a kitchen that was bedlam itself.

There was no satisfying them. Four times a day they ate their own weight in wet mash. Four times a day they sploshed and wallowed in their drinking water. Four times a day they sat down in it. Four times a day they turned their carefully tidied nursery boxes into fetid swamps, and four times a day we cleaned up after them. We were the body servants, and nursemaids of our ducks. All else went by the board. We were their slaves.

As the days passed, it became increasingly difficult for us to keep our growing ducklings in their box nurseries. They liked us. They wanted to be with us. Lucy became quite adept at skipping over them as she moved, with a hot frying pan, or pot of soup, between the kitchen stove and the kitchen sink. We put screens on their boxes, but they found a way through them. Never a mealtime went by but at least one of our twenty-five webb-footed friends made his way out of the kitchen, across the living room floor to our table.

"Peep," he would say. "Hi ya! Hi ya!"

We kept our ducklings with us as long as we could.

They were fun. It was only when Titch, our house cat, grew resentful of ducks that tried to swim in her milk dish that we decided, reluctantly, that the time had come for us to move our broad-billed little clowns out of their kitchen nursery into the larger, safer confines of the refurbished brooder.

"The Owl Pen will seem empty without them," I told Lucy.

"And fresher," Lucy told me.

The day we moved our ducklings from the kitchen to the brooder house, we gave them their food out of a big milk pan. They gulped nearly a bucketful of mash at each serving. Though only a month old, they tucked away at each meal more than our 287 Chanticler chicks ate in three. They gave up peeping. They quacked. They squeaked. In one short fortnight they outgrew the brooder house, and we put them out of it into a slatted pen on the hillside pasture field.

One morning we discovered that tiny, spreading patches of genuine feathers were to be seen quite plainly on their down-covered breasts and legs. Lucy and I said something approaching a prayer of thankfulness. We had lost many of our baby chicks during their first few critical weeks of life. We had lost none of our ducklings. With the appearance of these first feathers we knew that the dangers of babyhood which afflict ducklings as well as chicks, were all but past. Soon our ducklings, ducklings no longer, would waddle and strut in the full glory of their Rouen featherhood among the wildflowers on the hillside. Soon Owl Pen Pond would glow with the beauty of them swimming there like so many little painted galleons out of an old picture book.

The days passed, and the feathers grew. Lucy and I watched, at first eagerly, and then uneasily, and at last with open-mouthed alarm. Something was wrong, seriously wrong. Our ducks were not what our ducks should be. We checked with our duck book.

"The drake," said our book, "is a most splendid fellow, with a beautiful metallic green head, a claret-coloured breast, a white ring around his neck, and a body of soft French grey. A clearly defined band of rich blue, edged with white, crosses his wings. He has brick red legs and feet, and a bill of yellow-green, with a black bean at the tip . . . "

"The duck," our book continued, "has a bill of bright orange, tipped with black, a head of rich brown, and hazel eyes. A wider black band runs from the base of her bill to her neck, and up either side of her head to her eyes. Her body feathers are of a lovely brown, each feather being finely pencilled, and each wing carries a white-edged blue band, similar to that appearing on the wings of the drake. There is no white ring on the neck, and to have one is a defect."

Our duck breeder had obviously not read our book. Our youngsters were everything and anything that a Rouen should not be. They were black where they should have been white, and white where they should have been brown. They were grey where they should have been green, and brown where they should have been claret-coloured. Their fathers had not been what their fathers should have been. A moralist would have whispered that neither were their mothers.

"Perhaps," sighed Lucy, always the comforter, "perhaps if we stop calling them Rouens, and just think of them as nice fat little ducks it will be better for all of us."

It seemed the thing to do. The sins of the fathers had been visited upon the children, and there was no undoing it. We no longer talked of our Rouens. We no longer spoke of establishing a breeding flock of the "most beautiful of the utility type duck". We talked of our "quackers".

As time went on, we reconciled ourselves to their defects.
We even found ourselves ready to do battle with any un-
wary visitor who dared comment on their deficiencies. It
was not their fault that their mothers were fallen ducks.
Poor little devils! We made a song for the most impossible
of our ducklings, a piebald maiden with a black top-knot.
It began: "I'm Bella, da belle of da ball,

> White fedeers, an' top-knot, an' all . . . "

Our ducklings were six weeks old when we decided that
they were at last old enough to go swimming, old enough
to "take like a duck to water", and not die of it. We drove
them, protesting excitedly, from the green hillside, through
the garden gate, and down to the edge of Owl Pen Pond.
They saw water, in quantity, for the first time in their
lives. They saw it and stood transfixed, staring with bulging eyes and gaping bills.

Perhaps they found it hard to believe that this huge
pool of wetness, this great hunk of splashability, was real.
It is possible that they had come to think that water came
to mortal ducks only by the panful. Now a frog-filled
heaven of vast extent was suddenly spread before them.
It seemed too good, too damp to be true.

They stood like ships becalmed, like wooden decoy ducks,
entranced, drugged, hypnotized with delight. Not a duck
moved. Then, suddenly one of their number slid forward.
It was Bella. Down the bank she tumbled, head over heels.
The pond opened under her. She came up shouting. "Water,
Quack! Quack! It's real! Quack! Quack! It's wet." It
was the pure stuff of which ducks dream. Her joyous
yammering filled the air like a trumpet blast. The charm
was broken. The wooden images on the bank above her
galvanized into life, and poured down after her, over her,
a frantic cascade of webbed feet, broad bills, and thrashing wings.

There was no peace for the fish or frogs in Owl Pen

Pond that day. Our ducklings churned the water into a coffee-coloured foam. They spun in it like little feathered tops. They dived. They played at submarine. They played at squirt-me-and-I'll-squirt-you. They up-ended. They buried their heads in the mud of the pond bottom, and wriggled their fatuous little tails ecstatically in the air. They chased frogs, and they chased fish, and they chased each other.

They were tired little ducks that night.

# 24

## *We Deal With Teeth*

It was with something approaching a shock that Lucy and I came to realization of the fact that though we lived in a long-settled and civilized farming community, the wilderness was no farther from us than our nearest fence corner. We had thought that our first responsibility to our livestock was their feeding, and the cleaning of their pens. We found that it was something far more starkly elemental than that. A happy little pullet that had not noticed a red fox crouched in the stone pile by the dam, drove the lesson home to us. Protection was our problem. We were at war.

After we had tucked the mangled little body away among the grass roots under the birch tree, Lucy and I walked our fields and hedgerows, seeing them with new eyes. We looked at the wild flowers and thought not of their beauty, but of the sharp teeth they hid. We looked at the swaying rushes by the creek, and thought of the eyes that lurked among them. We looked again at the stone pile by the dam, and wondered what curved claw might still be resting in its heart, waiting for darkness, waiting to pounce.

"You know what we're doing?" I asked Lucy.

"Yes," said she. "We're seeing things from the point of view of our chickens and our ducks." She sighed. "It changes things, doesn't it?"

Actually our fight, though it took us a long time to recognize it as such, began the day our day-old chicks came to Owl Pen through the snowdrifts of March. As the days grew warmer, and the chicks older, we opened the brooder house window, and left it open. Our chicks grew timid, panicking wildly when we opened the brooder house door, and skuttering like little hunted things in a wild pell-mell race around the brooder stove when we came in. We could not understand their fear. We had done nothing to frighten them. We went to our books for an explanation and found none. At last we noticed some long, thin scratches on the brooder house window sill.

"Screen it," advised a friend who had long years of experience in the raising of poultry. "Take off the muslin you have on, and nail on heavy wire. Don't be like me. I put fly-screen on my brooder house window, and an old man racoon came along and tore it off like tissue paper. He killed two hundred and fifty of my birds in one night. Put heavy screen on your brooder house window, and nail it down with spikes."

We took his advice, and the exploring raccoon, or mink, or fox, or whatever it was, drew his claws no longer over the window-sill. Our chicks became quiet again, and welcomed us, as of old, with happy cheeping instead of panic-stricken screams, when we visited them. But it wasn't peace that we had achieved. The wilderness was still with us, and the only peace it offered was an uneasy interval between one fight and the next.

The time came when it was necessary for us to take our chicks out of the brooder house and put them into little red-roofed range shelters that we had set up on the hillside. Put them out we did, and twice, three times, and even four times a day, for days afterwards, we found them crouched in terror in the shadows of the shelters, hiding from tiny specks that wheeled and hovered in the sky above—hawks.

The hawks were, quite probably, of a harmless species. Most hawks are harmless to chickens, and are, indeed, valuable to the countryman for the vermin they kill, but our chicks did not know that. Their instinct told them to beware of hawks, to fear and hide from anything that passed or hung overhead. So hide they did. Once again they grew panicky and jumpy. A lonely blackbird flying over the pasture field was enough to send every last one of them racing in headlong, squeaking terror, for the nearest cover. I brought out my gun, and wasted a box of ammunition and a whole forenoon shooting at specks in the upper blue. A city naturalist, with no chickens to tend, wrote regretting my shooting at "such harmless predators". I had my regrets—that I had missed the bloody things.

Friends came visiting, and told us how much they envied us our rural quiet, and our rural peace. Lucy and I were not impressed. We knew the price we paid for our peace —our seeming peace—and quiet—days of work in our fields with hammers, and snare wires, and traps—nights spent with one ear wide awake, with a flashlight on the window-sill, and a loaded gun by the door. They spoke of the pioneers, and chanted praise of these hardy folk, telling how they had driven back the wilderness, changing Medonte from a jungle of pine trees and cedar swamps into the peaceful farmlands of to-day. They talked of the pioneers driving back the wilderness, and while they talked Lucy and I bent in our pasture field, studying little paths that wound in a circle around our range shelters, paths that had been made at night, and by neither our chickens nor ourselves. We knew how far the pioneers had pushed back the wilderness—so did our chickens.

Our ducks, too, had a very clear picture of the real significance of that buccolic peace of which the city poets sing. They knew, as we knew, that the wilderness was biding its time with them, waiting, watching, ready to spring the moment a chance was given. They were tasty little morsels, big for their age, well-fleshed and fat, just what a mother fox or mink might dream of taking home to her den.

One evening, as Lucy and I sat on the bank above Moonstone Creek watching our broad-billed youngsters frolic and up-end in the water below, we saw them suddenly stop in their play, quack loudly, and then dash frantically, with thrashing wings and gaping bills, towards the broader, deeper, safer water of the pond. For a moment we were puzzled. There was, so far as we could see, nothing on the water or in the water to frighten our little flock. We looked again. We saw a tiny dimple in the water, a dimple that grew as we watched, into a speeding, arrow-shaped streak that followed our ducks downstream towards the pond mouth. It disappeared, appeared again and was gone.

We don't know what made that moving ripple on the still surface of our stream. It might have been the snout of a submerged mink. It might have been made by the nose of a muskrat, by a turtle, or a snake. Whatever it was, our ducks feared it, and that was enough for us. We hurried our web-footed babes off the pond and into their sleeping pen, resolving that from that time on, they would always be off the pond and into their sleeping quarters before deepening twilight brought the wilderness creeping under our line fence, or swimming down our gurgling stream, to threaten that which was ours.

For awhile our ducks seemed to agree with us. Every night, for weeks on end, they came at our twilight call, waddling obediently up the steep bank from the water, filing like little soldiers through the narrow gap that was the entrance to their sleeping pen. Every night, night after night, we counted them in, and tucked them in, and locked the slat-pen door. We congratulated ourselves on having such well-behaved, such well-disciplined ducks, but we congratulated ourselves too soon.

There came a night when our ducks, like any other children, grew tired of being good. Lucy found me at the
pond side, red with anger, and hoarse with calling, hopelessly cursing the sweet little darlings, who were gathered
in a derisive group on the water below. I had spent a
good half-hour quacking the invitation that had always
brought them skedaddling to bed. I had quacked until I
could quack no more, and the little beasts had refused to
budge. I had thrown sticks and stones into the water
beside them, hoping to frighten them off, and they had
gurgled with delight. I had barked like a fox, and yapped
like a mink. Neighbours passing on the nearby concession
line had heard, and had gone on their way, shaking their
heads sadly. The ducks had ignored me completely.

"Leave them alone," advised Lucy. "They'll come off
the water of their own accord as soon as it is really dark."

I left them alone. Darkness, real darkness, came to the
Owl Pen, and the Owl Pen pond. There was not even a
star in the sky. A bat squeaked. A whip-poor-will sang.
The ducks still quacked on the pond.

"Be patient," said Lucy, and went to bed.

I was patient. The long minutes crept by. I grew tired
of being patient. I grew tired of waiting. It was midnight.
I went to the pond-side and saw our ducks, mere blacker
blackness in the general blackness, still swimming. I weighed
my alternatives. I could stand guard on the pond-side
all night; I could go to bed and chance the re-appearance
of that ominous arrow headed ripple; I could peel off my
clothes and go in after them, mud, stones, weeds, darkness, and all.

I undressed. I stripped to the hide, except for my socks,
which I left on to protect my feet from the dark-hidden
boulders with which the pond bottom was strewn. I waded
gingerly in. Of course I slipped. Of course I fell. The
inky black waters of Owl Pen Pond closed over my frantic

head. I floundered. I lost my socks, both of them. I found my feet and stood up, chin deep in shivery spring water, just in time to see the last of our web-footed darlings, our blasted ducks, waddle solemnly up the bank and into the pen.

For one wild moment I prayed that some handy spirit of the night would change me into a giraffe. For one wild moment I would have given ten years of my life, just for a neck long enough to enable me to reach out from where I stood and snap that last duck in two. I was at that moment myself the wilderness incarnate, red in tooth and claw, and stubbed big toe.

# PART 9

## Trouble Has Four Feet

*I think that I shall never see*
*A skunk with equanimity.*

OLD TATTERED MSS.

# 25

## *We Become Goat Herders*

OUR NEW MILK SUPPLY CAME TO US IN THE BACK SEAT OF a friend's car, tense with excitement, and grumbling softly. It came sitting bolt upright, with an insistent dignity, a determined pomposity that was almost human. It came in the shape of two dappled nanny goats, two scrawny, couple-coloured beauties, with lovely eyes, and a hippy angularity that reminded us, peculiarly enough, of school marms and missionaries. We reached in through the open car window and scratched their tremulous chins. They ba-a-hed their thanks. We thought them elegant.

"Our troubles are over," declared Lucy, thinking of winter storms, and springtime mud, and the long, up-hill walk to Plum Tree Farm, where we had been getting our milk.

"Maybe," murmured our friend, her eyes dancing with laughter, laughter that we did not quite like, or at the time, understand. "We'll talk about that when you have had the little beasties for awhile." She proceeded to introduce us to our new charges. "The bigger goat is Suzanne, and she is not too good a milker. The smaller goat is Josephine, and she is doing quite well. It has been said that they are not easy to milk, and that they have a way with fences. It has been said that they are the sort to provoke angels to profanity." She considered us a moment in thoughtful silence. "You may have your hands full." She started up her car again. "I wish you luck," she said, and was gone.

Lucy and I were left alone with our goats. It would have been nice to have had a place to put them, but we didn't. We had no goat barn at all, and the piece of cross-creek pasture, which was not occupied by our wild geese, and which was to be their special kingdom, was not yet fenced. We had, however, a fine new chicken house, and a yet unused chicken run. We decided to put them there.

"It will be easy," I told Lucy as we heaved our excited and unwilling nannies through the wire gate leading to the run. "They can pasture here until we find time to get a fence around their proper stamping ground. We'll put a couple of tie rings in the chicken house wall, a nice thick layer of pine shavings on the floor, a brace of buckets for water and chop, and a basket for hay handy, and there you are."

"It sounds easy," agreed Lucy, and then a little dubiously, "it sounds too easy."

"Nonsense," said I.

We set to work. Lucy collected buckets and food, and spread the golden shavings two inches thick on the cement floor of the chicken house. I busied myself fastening two steel rings to the whitewashed wall, passing stout ropes through them, and making all ready for the tenants to be.

We even, in an excess of enthusiasm, nailed a great spray of pine needles to the slanting ceiling. It looked nice. We admired our handiwork, and then turned to collect our goats.

We hadn't far to go. We turned to find them standing in the chicken house doorway, regarding us solemnly. It seems that they were lonely in their strange new Owl Pen world. They had not liked our chicken run. They had wanted company, and so they had casually sailed over our five-foot-high chicken fence, barbed wire top and all, and come visiting.

"Easy," said Lucy, smiling evily.

"Bah!" said I.

"Ba-a-a-h!" said our goats.

We put them back into the chicken run, and they came out again, over the fence top, as we watched. We put them in a third time, and when they crouched for a third spring, we opened the gate hurriedly and went in to them. That seemed to satisfy them. They nuzzled us a bit, murmured contentedly, and then went about their proper business of eating the new grass in the run. When we turned to leave, they left off eating, and followed us to the gate. When we shut the gate in their faces, they waggled their tails, eyed the fence top, and crouched again to leap. It was quite apparent that our goats had no intention at all of staying alone in our chicken pen. We took them into the chicken house, and tied them with the new ropes to the whitewashed wall.

I wasn't particularly perturbed. Somewhere among our books, I remembered, was a statement by a world authority, to the effect that an electric fence, while utterly incapable of injuring even a mouse, will hold a stallion, a bull, or even an elephant, prisoner behind its one frail strand of wire. The book, as I remembered it, went on to say that no beast that had once suffered a shock or two from such a fence, would ever again approach within feet of it.

We sent by truck to the village of Coldwater for the best electric fence to be had in the general store there. We drove long lines of stakes into the borders of our cross-creek pasture, and screwed insulator knobs to them. We strung a line of bright new wire, and then remembering that we were building to hold not bulls, or stallions, or elephants, but two small goats, strung a second wire under it. Then, just to be on the safe side, we ran a third charged wire around our field. One line, our book said would hold a pachyderm. Three lines, I felt sure, would hold our goats. We led them into the field and turned them loose. They nosed the wire, and leaped wildly away from it, bawling a protest that scared the crows from the elm trees. Lucy and I marched back to the Owl Pen, a conquering army of two.

It was nice of our goats to allow us this moment of supreme self-satisfaction. It was a pity that they had to take the edge off it at milking time. It took the two of us to hold the smaller of them, Josephine. She did everything but turn inside out in her frantic efforts to keep her teats away from our hands. She reared, she bucked, she kicked, she lay down on them. Yet milk her we did, in a shower of milk that spattered everywhere except into the pail. Suzanne was as bad, or worse, for she managed to put her black foot squarely into the milk pail. Our goats were panting, and we were too exhausted to pant, when the job was done. Still, we had a quart and a half of stepped-in milk to show for our labour.

"It's the first of many quarts," I told Lucy.

"It's the first of many milkings," moaned she.

The next day we put our pair of nannies back into the cross-creek pasture, back behind the electric fence. They stayed there, like lambs, and our spirits rose. They had even, without too much argument, submitted to the morning milking. We felt like bragging a bit of our prowess, of our way with goats, and so telephoned their former owner to tell of our success. We invited her to come and see how well an electric fence would hold a goat. She came. Our goats bawled recognition, and marched straight through our bull-elephant-stallion-holding fence to meet her. Our visitor was a very understanding sort of woman. She did not even smile at us. She said little, and she left soon.

"The power must be off," I exploded, as soon as she was gone. "It must be for those puny little brutes to walk through our fence like that. Why, the book says . . . "

"The power is on," insisted Lucy.

"It can't be."

"It is."

"You mean to stand there and tell me that a blistering pair of nanny goats will go where a great, big bull wouldn't dare?" I stormed. "Look," I shouted, "I'll show you." I reached for the top wire of the fence.

"Don't," warned Lucy.

"Nonsense," said I.

I grabbed the top wire. An invisible devil kicked me in the teeth. My toes turned suddenly up like bent spikes. My heart did a sommersault. The power was on. I rubbed my hands on my trousers, and looked at our goats with reluctant admiration.

"See," said Lucy.

I saw. I marched up the hill to Plum Tree Farm and borrowed Farmer Jim's electric fencer. I took it off a single wire in his back pasture where he had been using it to hold a whole herd of beef cattle. Back to the Owl Pen I carried it, and hooked it to our fence beside our machine, and turned both machines on high. Josephine rubbed up to the doubly-charged fence, shook as the current hit her, and bawled frantically. Suzanne nosed where Jo had rubbed, and leaped wildly backwards. Remembering what a single charge had done to me, I clucked sympathetically.

With a that-will-hold-you grin on our faces, Lucy and I left our nannies behind their double-charged, three-wire, electric fence, and went back over the dam to the Owl Pen. Suzanne, dripping wet, met us on the lawn. She had swum the creek, which is one boundry of the pasture, and which we had felt sure would hold water-hating goats—even our goats—to the crack of doom. We led her back across the creek and put her back into the pasture, where Jo, excited by Sue's desertion of her, was bawling in a paroxysm of loneliness.

Once again we started for home. We started, and we stopped. There was a commotion behind us. We looked back to see Jo, four feet in the air, sailing over the fence in a graceful, sky-climbing leap. Suzanne, still wet from the creek, and bawling lustily as the current hit her, was crawling under the fence. We caught Jo, almost as she landed, and we caught Sue as she wriggled free of the fence. They wanted to be petted. We petted them. And then we put a poke, an arrangement of crossed sticks around the neck of Sue, and a strong web hobble on Jo.

A poke is supposed, according to the best authorities, to make it impossible for any living thing to get through even an ordinary wire fence. A hobble is supposed, according to the same authorities, to make it impossible for even a gazelle to jump over a soap box. Our fence was not ordinary. It was charged with high tension electricity. Our fence was over a yard high. Our goats, hobbled and poked as they were, went over, and under, and through it, without any trouble at all. They sailed. They slithered. They bawled. And that was all there was to it. They wanted some more petting, it seemed. Wearily, we petted them again.

We were beaten, and we knew it. We put them back

into the pasture, for the umpteenth time, closed the charged gate on them, and returned hopelessly to Owl Pen. At any moment we expected to hear our blasted goats blatting behind us. Our milk supply was in a state of open mutiny, and we could do nothing about it. We thought of calling up the friend who had given the beasts to us, imploring her to come and take them away. We thought of guns, and knives, and hangman's nooses.

Some little time passed before it oozed into our gloom-soaked minds that our she-devil nanny goats had actually not followed us on this, our latest trip from the cross-creek pasture home. Incredibly, all was quiet across the creek. No frantic hoofs were stamping behind us on the grey plank bridge over the dam. We hurried to a vantage point, and looked back across the creek to the pasture. Maybe our goats were dead—electrocuted. They weren't. We saw them, with eyes that popped with utter unbelief, grazing contentedly the herbage they had so long scorned.

It wasn't victory that we had achieved. It wasn't even peace. It was, we discovered as the days passed, a sort of truce, an uneasy sort of truce imposed not by us on our goats, but by our goats on us. So long as we left them completely undisturbed in the pasture, so long as we kept away from them, and kept visitors away from them, they would stay in their cross-creek pasture. They would stay there between the hours of seven o'clock in the morning when we milked them and put them there, and seven o'clock at night when, it developed, they were accustomed to being milked again and put in a barn. If we tried to put them in the pasture before seven in the morning, they promptly came out of it. If we neglected to go for them by seven o'clock at night, they came for us. It was not a matter for argument. It was seven to seven—take it or leave it.

We took it.

# 26

*We Pay the Piper*

LUCY AND I HAD ALWAYS SUPPOSED THAT OUR FIRST
market day would be a red letter day in our lives. It would
mark Owl Pen's coming of age, we had told ourselves a
dozen times. When that day came, we would at long last
be able to take our place beside our neighbours, true
countrymen indeed. In our dreams we saw ourselves riding
to town with great brown crates of fine white cockerels,
and fat ducks piled behind us. We saw ourselves pulling
into the yard of the local co-operative, nodding to friends
who had come with their produce, smiling at the manager
who had come rushing out to meet us. And always, in
our dreams, we heard him whispering to his helper.

"Must be nice to these folk—these Owl Pen folk. Their
poultry is the fattest and the finest in the land."

That is the way we dreamed it, and it wasn't like that
at all. We didn't enjoy our first market day. We hated
it, and we hated ourselves. We felt like going into the
local police station and giving ourselves up as foul murderers who had no right to walk in the sun, or talk with
decent folk. We wondered that the co-op manager deigned
to speak to us at all, and we would not have been at all
surprised if our friends had crossed the road, as we came
down the street, in order to avoid meeting us.

Our feeling of despondency and low-downess began at
dawn at the Owl Pen, at the very beginning of the great
day to which we had so long looked forward. It started
when we began loading forty-six fat cockerels, and eleven
fat ducks into slatted crates, and it did not end for weeks

afterwards. Into those crates went Joe Dokes, a husky
young cockerel who had lost five toes in a brooder house
brawl months before, and who had spent weeks as an in-
valid in a box in the Owl Pen kitchen, and more weeks as
a sort of house guest on the Owl Pen doorstep and lawn.
Among the ducks that we loaded was Bella, beautiful Bella
of the black top-knot, about whom we had written a poem.

We loaded the crates feeling like murderers, and it was
cold comfort at best for us to tell ourselves that it was
our own stupid fault for making pets of our livestock.
We had named them. We had nursed them, and babied
them, and petted them. We had treated them almost like
children, and, at times, had almost thought of them as such.
Our farmer neighbours had warned us, and had told us
tales of upsets that had been caused in their families by
the marketing of named birds and animals, but we had
not listened. We were paying the piper for our foolishness.

It wasn't so bad loading the cockerels, though it was, in
all conscience, bad enough. Lucy's face was set. There
was no smile in her eyes. I handed the struggling birds
out of the fattening pen to her, and she put them into a
crate that we had drawn up on a wheelbarrow, to the fattening pen door. We didn't look at each other, and we
didn't speak to each other. We didn't dare. I think that
as we worked, we were both thanking our lucky stars that
our cockerels had, by their constant fighting and trouble
making during the past month, somewhat cooled our liking
for them.

But there was Joe Dokes, poor, battle-scarred Joe. I
picked him up and handed him, without comment, out to
Lucy, hoping that she would not notice the toeless feet
that identified him. She missed nothing. She glanced at
me, swallowed hard, and thrust him hurriedly into the
crate. We had to be practical . . . had to be practical.

Slowly the pen emptied. Slowly the crate filled. We kept thinking of Joe.

The loading of the ducks was an even worse experience. We really liked our ducks. The barnyard knows no happier, harmless, lovable creature than a duck. Ducks never fight. Ducks never pull each other's toes off. Ducks are gossipy and frolicsome. Standing on their heads in pond water, wiggling their ridiculous little bottoms in the air, they are a cure for any man's blues.

It was with leaden feet that we at last wheeled the barrow to the duck pen door. Had we been able to afford it, we would have chucked barrow and crate together down the steep bank into the pond. We would have opened the pen door and set all our quackers free. But ducks, for all their endearing ways, and real loveliness, eat like little feathered pigs, and feed is expensive. We could not afford to keep them—not all of them.

We had considered shipping the whole twenty-five of them, for they were too mixed in their breeding to be useful to us as breeding stock, and they were at the proper marketing age of ten weeks. They were big, fat, and healthy. But the thought of our pond, silent again, and empty of the proud little frog-hunting flotilla that had for so long lorded it over our part of Moonstone Creek, was too much. We decided to ship half of them, and to keep half of them, until September at least.

Fate would have it that Bella should be among the first that came to my hand in the crowded pen. Lucy took her from me, gulped audibly and thrust her into the slatted box on the barrow.

"Ken . . . "

"Yes?"

"I don't like being a farmer . . . "

At that moment, neither did I. I handed her another duck . . . another . . . and another. All that we were planning to ship were loaded at last, all but one. I reached for it, a piebald drake, caught it, and handed it to Lucy. Someone fumbled. It may have been Lucy. It may have been I. The drake squeaked loudly, slithered from our hands, and was free. Down the steep bank it tumbled, through the sedges to the water.

"I'm glad he got away," said Lucy defiantly, "I'm glad, and I'm not going to help you catch him."

I didn't ask her to.

We stood in silence watching our gleefully squeaking escapee join his comrades, who had been on the pond since daybreak. We watched them gather around him, quacking, gossiping. We watched the pathetically shrunken little fleet drift round a bend and disappear from view.

Silly, isn't it?

But that's the way it was.

A few days later a friend came with a box and added three pretty wild mallards to our flock.

# 27

*We Raise a Stink*

THE EVENING MIGHT HAVE ENDED AS PEACEFULLY AS IT had begun, if Lucy had not gone to the north door to empty a teapot among the rose bushes. Even then, all might have been well had she not just chanced to look down into the valley where our fifty white hives stood gleaming like so many pallid tombstones in the dusk.

"Pst," she whispered.

"Pst, yourself," I told her, and kept my eyes in my book.

"Skunk," she whispered.

That did it. We had been watching for weeks past for the striped pirate that had been raiding our bee-yard. Skunks are not welcome there. They like bees too well. They eat them, scooping them by the black paw from the fronts of the hives, cramming them into their voracious black mouths in such numbers as to cause even strong colonies to dwindle, in the course of a few weeks of repeated visits, into nothingness. Already we had lost three colonies to these night-prowling bee thieves. Every morning for weeks past we had found our hive fronts scratched and muddied by their greedy paws. Now our chance for vengeance was at hand.

I got my gun and loaded it. Very carefully I opened the door. Very carefully I stepped out into the deepening twilight. I saw the flick of a black and white tail as the marauder in the valley sat up for a better look at me. I thrust the gun to my shoulder. I felt Lucy's breath on my right ear. I fired.

Even as I pressed the trigger I knew I was going to miss.

162

All thoughts of skunk-killing went out of my mind. My one thought as the gun roared and the bullet went crashing into the valley below was for our hives. Where was that bullet going? I saw the skunk saunter calmly away among the cedars. I heard Lucy shouting at me to shoot again. I didn't. I didn't care anything at all about that old skunk.

I ran down the hill with my heart in my mouth. Where had that bullet gone? Through an expensive hive? Through hard-won combs of honey? Through massed thousands of bees? Had it killed a queen? I galloped about the bee-yard, examining hive after hive. There was no hole in this one. There was no hole in that one. There was no hole in any of them. There was no evidence of any kind in the bee-yard to suggest that I had fired at all.

I came out of the valley relieved at finding that I had done no damage, but at the same time feeling rather silly. I had fired at a skunk in a bee-yard and missed a whole apiary. Still, the light was bad. The shadows were deep. The skunk was mostly black. I looked at Lucy. She didn't say anything. She didn't grin. She just looked at me. My alibi died on my lips.

Next morning I got up early, did my chores, milked my goats, fed my chickens, brushed my hair and went to town. I wanted poison, strong poison, skunk poison. Into a drug store I marched.

"Give me strychnine," I told the clerk, "six lethal doses."

"Lethal doses?" the clerk inquired, somewhat timidly I thought.

"Man killing doses," I replied, and noticed her eyebrows twitch. "You see," I explained, "I want to kill a skunk, and some skunks take some killing." The clerk seemed to be having trouble with her chin. "I can't afford to take any chances," I continued brightly, "there is a certain element of self-respect involved in this . . . "

"Self-respect?" sighed the clerk.

"Nothing but," I insisted. "My wife doesn't think . . . "
Somewhat puzzled, I watched the clerk scuttle suddenly
out of the shop into the private regions in the rear. I
heard a sound of whispering.

The proprietor scuttled in.

"You were wanting strychnine," he inquired softly, from
the depths of a glass-fronted cage at the end of the counter.

"Yes," I replied.

"In lethal doses," he whispered.

"Yes."

"What for?" he shouted.

I almost jumped out of my skin.

"For a skunk!" I shouted back.

"What kind of skunk?" he quavered.

"A bee-eating skunk," I growled. "A smelly, stripe-
tailed skunk." A light dawned. "Say . . . "

"Never mind," sighed the druggist, and waved his hand
as though after a fly. Out of the corner of my eye I saw
a burly man in shirt sleeves turn away from the shop window. He might have been a casual passerby, and he
might not have been. I got my strychnine, signed the
poison book, and got out of town.

My plan of attack was all written down for me in a
government bulletin. As a prelude to, and perhaps as a
sort of justification for, the cold-blooded instructions for
murder that it gives, the bulletin begins by stressing the
fact that skunks are troublesome, that they annoy bees,
and eat bees, destroying whole colonies. It then continues:

"The control recommended for skunks is to make a small
hole in an egg in the air sack end. Then stir one grain
of strychnine well into the egg with a toothpick, or small
piece of wire. The egg is then half buried near the hive
where the skunk can get it . . . "

I doctored the eggs as directed, and laid them out in

a row on the kitchen table. They looked very nice. I closed my eyes and saw skunks, dead skunks, laid in a long line across country, from the Owl Pen to the very door of the Ministry of Agriculture. Just before twilight, I took the poisoned eggs into the bee-yard and set them in the grass between the hives.

For the rest of the evening Lucy and I stood at the north door of the Owl Pen, with our noses bent sideways on the fly screen. We stood their waiting, hoping that our friend the skunk would turn up before it got too dark for us to see the show, and sample the treat we had prepared for him. The minutes ticked by. Two hours passed, and our necks and legs grew stiff.

"There he is," said Lucy.

Sure enough, there by the alighting board of the first of our hives he stood, white-striped tail and all. He sniffed at the egg that was there, and then ignored it. He apparently liked bees better. He skipped over my second poisoned egg like a ballet dancer skipping over a stage mushroom. He moved to a second hive, and the third egg, toyed with it like a pup toying with a bone, tossed it to one side, and gulped down more of our bees. I gritted my teeth. It was for this that I had gone to town and scared a druggist's clerk half out of her lovely skin. It was for this that I had spoiled half-a-dozen eggs. It was too much.

I got my gun again, and loaded it. I knew there was no point in my trying to sneak up on the brute. He would hear the screen door open sure as Fate. I flung silence and caution to the winds. I banged open the screen door. I barged down the hillside like a locomotive gone mad. My thought was to get into the bee-yard before the rattled skunk could get out of it. I did. I aimed. I fired. I think I hit him. I heard Lucy cheering, and laughing too, I think.

I caught a glimpse of a flicking tail, as the stripe-tailed devil disappeared again among the cedars. I dashed after him, lost him in the shadows, and then had the joyful experience of having him scramble over my feet as I stood by a fallen tree, debating what direction I should go in search of him. I fired again, mercifully missing my toes. The skunk dived for a nearby hole. I fired again, and again, and again. The air filled with a blue haze. At first I thought it was powder smoke. Then I knew that it was not. My nose crinkled. My eyes burned. I dropped my gun. I fled up the hillside.

"I got him, Lucy! I got him!" I gasped.

"You're telling me," said she, and shut the door in my face.

"But Lucy . . . "

"Phooey!"

"Let me in," I pleaded.

"Go 'way," she snorted. "You . . . you . . . you petunia!"

I'd have saved myself a lot of trouble if I'd eaten those eggs myself.

# PART 10

## Bitter Sweet

*"To live on a farm and enjoy all that it has to offer is the greatest good that can be attained by poet or a philosopher..."*

PETER McArthur, 1925

# 28

## *We Harvest Honey*

IN THE OLD DAYS, BEE MASTERS TALKED OF TELLING THE bees. If anything of importance happened in the household of a bee master, the bees had to be told. If someone died, the bees were told. If a son was born, the bees were told. If the red cow freshened, and gave birth to twin heifer calves, one of the household had to go down into the bee-yard and striding solemnly from hive to hive, tell the buzzing occupants the news. It was said, and believed, that to neglect this chore would be to offend the bees, so that they would either swarm and leave the place, or else sulk in their hives and refuse to make honey.

Lucy and I told our bees nothing. It was not that we lacked respect for the old belief. It was simply that our bees had no time for our chitter-chatter. They were busy.

When there was any telling to be done, they did it. They told us. And Lucy and I learned quickly to listen in silence, and with respect.

I do believe that it was this willingness of ours to listen to our bees, and to follow their dictates with a certain energetic humbleness, that brought our first season with bees to such an unexpectedly successful conclusion. We listened, and we learned to understand what we heard, and we did as we were told. That was all there was to it. We attempted no manipulation of our colonies. We didn't know how. We let them manipulate us. In the springtime when they yelled for food, we fed them. When they cried their loss of a queen, we gave them a new queen. When they rumbled uneasily because of the midnight assaults of mice, or toads, or skunks, we disposed of mice, and toads, and skunks. When they sang their harvest song, we took the hint and gave them room for their harvest. And in between times, we left them severely alone.

The bright days of summer slipped by. Day after day, week after week, our bees flew back and forth over the Owl Pen roof, filling their hives to bursting point with the rich, golden sweetness of the Medonte fields. Day after day, week after week, Lucy and I bent over our benches, striving to keep pace with our bees, to keep them supplied with supers and combs sufficient to their needs. The one demand from our roaring hives was for room, more room. Lucy worked like a galley slave in her studio, nailing bee frames together, fitting them with metal eyelets, wiring them with four tightly stretched wires, fastening bright sheets of beeswax into them. She made a hundred. She made five hundred. She made a thousand. She made two thousand. I worked at the supers, the box-like structures that were to hold them. I assembled supers. I fitted supers with their bits and pieces. I painted and re-painted supers, giving them three coats of glistening white paint.

Stacks of the things grew like mushrooms in the workyard, and yet the demand was always for three or ten more. Though we worked night and day we never succeeded in quite quieting that bee-yard cry for room.

Then, suddenly, the shouting died. An almost breathless hush crept over the bee-yard. The vast armada of tiny fliers that for days and weeks on end had filled the air above the Owl Pen with the flash of brilliant wings was no more to be seen. Lucy looked up from her frame-making with a sigh of relief. I put down my hammer. The honey flow was over. The fields, though still flower-starred, were empty of bees.

With a prayer of thankfulness in our hearts, Lucy and I stood on the little hill above our bee-yard looking at the checker board of white hives spread out below. We had started in the spring ignorant, except for our reading, of even the rudiments of bee-keeping, with fifty three-pound packages of bees. Having no comb, we had hived them on plain sheets of beeswax, and hoped for the best. Somehow, forty-five of the fifty packages had survived our bungling, and had grown into strong colonies. Our squat white hives had grown into skyscrapers. They stood in our bee-yard, tiered three and four and five supers high, and holding, according to our estimate, nearly two tons of fine white clover honey.

All that remained was the harvesting. All we had to do now was to take our honey from our honey bees. That was all. I gulped. In my mind's eye I saw myself backing slowly across the bee-yard, giving ground inch by inch, battling it out in a toe-to-toe slugging match with some two million fighting mad bees. I looked at Lucy. She shook her head.

"Don't look at me," she said. "I've just decided that a woman's place is in the home, with the door shut."

I needed help, strong-backed expert help, and so I called

a friend who lived in the next township, a man with many years of bee-keeping experience.

"You'll have everything ready?" he asked, when I had explained my need.

"Everything."

"Right," he agreed, "I'll come."

My helper came expecting to find that I had, days earlier, placed bee escape boards, hive-sized squares of plywood fitted with one-way bee gates, under the honey supers. Had I done so, the bees would have gone down out of the supers, through the bee gates, and would have been unable to return. The supers would have been empty of bees. But I had put none on. Bees filled the supers and spread in a thick, living carpet over every honey-comb.

"Why didn't you tell me you had no bee escape boards?" he asked, after a quick glance into one roaring stack.

"But I have," I protested.

"Where?" he grunted.

"In the storage shed."

"Well," said my helper. "Well." He scratched his head, and looked at me with a queer, pitying expression on his face.

I hastened to reassure him. I wasn't mad. Not really. Nor had I been careless. I had a way of clearing bees out of a honey super that made bee escape boards as obsolete as a hoop skirt, as old-fashioned as a bustle. He looked interested. I told him of reading in my bee books that bees hated the smell of carbolic acid, that all a man had to do to rid his honey supers, in a matter of minutes, of every last bee, was sprinkle a solution of carbolic on a cloth, and spread it over the combs.

"Just like that," he grunted.

"Just like that," I insisted.

"I'm willing to learn," said my helper, "bring out your dope."

Very much the master of the situation, I brought out my brown bottle of acid and water. I sprinkled a cloth with it. I took the cover from a super top. The bees welled up in the dark, murmuring, honey-defending flood. I drew the soaked cloth over them.

"That's all there is to it," I crowed.

"Brother," murmured my friend. "Brother, you had better be right."

Three minutes passed, and it was time, according to the book, to take the cloth from the super top. To leave it there longer would be to chance tainting the honey, or killing the bees. With that bland smile of smug superiority which the proud possessor of the newest and latest always delights to bestow on the stick-in-the-mud who clings to the out-moded and out-worn, I lifted my magic cloth.

"Look," I said proudly.

"Look yourself," yelled my helper. "The damned things are eating the stuff!"

So they were. Something was wrong. Tens of thousands of excited furiously fanning bees were welling out of the super top in the wake of the lifted cloth. The carbolic hadn't affected them a bit. Maybe they hadn't read the book. Certainly they were not afraid of the acid, not as I had mixed it.

"This shouldn't happen," I insisted.

My helper opened his mouth, and then, with a savage pop, closed it again. His hands shook. I did not like the look in his eyes. He picked up his smoker, and motioned to me to pick up mine. I picked it up thinking the while that it was very kind of him to say nothing. I did not know till later that the one thing that kept him quiet was a certain difficulty he was experiencing in finding just the right words. The presence of Lucy on the side hill above us limited his choice.

At last he ventured four short words.

"We'll brush them off," he said, and was straight away silent again.

Brush them off we did, ten upon tens of thousands of angry bees from tens upon tens of heavy, honey-loaded frames of glistening comb. We took the frames one at a time, from the roaring, bee-choked supers, and went over them with a long, white bristled brush. We brushed each comb until the last clinging, outraged, fighting mad bee fell from it, and then we tucked it into an empty, board-covered box. When the box was filled we trundled it away on the red wheelbarrow to the honey house.

All afternoon we heaved and brushed, and trundled, and groaned. The hum of the bee-yard changed into a tumultuous howl of rage and protest that drowned the burble of Moonstone Creek. Great crawling mounds of bees grew in the grass in front of every hive, and moved in a broad black curtain up their fronts. The hours rushed over us. We reloaded, and relit our smokers, washed our bee brushes clean of clogging honey, and smoked and brushed again. We took turns staggering between the bee-yard and the honey house with the red wheelbarrow moving over a hundredweight of honey every trip.

"Not bad at all," I gasped, elated beyond rhyme or reason by the growing pile of honey-filled supers that crowded the honey house. "Not bad at all!"

"Not bad at all!" whooped Lucy from the safety of the side hill.

My helper said nothing. What he had to say he saved until Lucy had gone indoors to make tea, and until the job was done. Then he said his say.

# 29

## *We Argue With Bees*

LUCY AND I WERE ABOUT TO EXPERIENCE THE CROWNING glory of our first season of bee-keeping. We were about to extract. We tied on our aprons, and proudly surveyed the great pile of honey comb that we had, with the help of a bee-keeping friend, brought into the honey house from the bee-yard. We chortled and sang as we made a last minute examination of our new extracting equipment, our shining new power extractor, our fat electric motor, our gleaming copper steam generator, our yawning storage tanks. All was in readiness. We tightened a belt here, screwed down a grease cup there, straightened a steam hose, and fingered our lovely new electric uncapping plane. We paid no attention at all to the single lonely bee that somewhere in the little building, was buzzing dolefully. Our house was bee-tight. What did one bee matter?

Lucy picked a fat comb out of the nearest super, and carried it across the room to the uncapping meter, a steam heated gadget built to receive and separate the mixture of wax and honey that falls from the uncapping plane as a comb is opened. I tested the sharp edge of the uncapping plane. It was hot.

"Now?" said Lucy.

"Now," said I.

Ours was the pride and delight of high priests at a pagan shrine. Solemnly I drew the hot edge of the plane across the shining white face of the comb. We gasped in unison. The uncovering of the golden sweetness within was like the unveiling of a goddess. It was beautiful. The air filled with a heady fragrance as honey and wax mingled and hissed on the hot knife edge. We were elated, elated as eagles in a thunder cloud, and quite as stupid. We saw no portent, read no omen, in the single bee that danced out of nowhere to alight, quivering with excitement, on the honey we had laid bare.

"Drink your fill, little fellow," we told him, and when he had drunk his fill, to the point of bursting, we carried him to the honey house door and shooed him away. "Go home," we simpered, "go back to your hive, but don't tell your pals where you've been."

We returned to our uncapping. Three bees lit on the next comb that we uncapped. Seven followed the edge of my plane across the third gleaming comb that we picked up. By the time we had finished uncapping thirty-eight combs, thus filling our extractor, several dozen wildly excited bees were buzzing over the uncapping melter. Several dozen more were exploring the whitewashed ceiling, and at least three were in my hair.

"They must have come in with the supers," I told Lucy. "It's nothing to worry about."

"No," she agreed uncertainly. "Not much."

We ignored the bees. We had something more important to do than worry about the presence of a few dozen buzzing honey hunters. Lucy reached up over the work bench and closed an electric switch. Our big electric motor howled. Belts whined. Pulleys chattered. I shoved home the iron clutch on the extractor. The heavy, comb-laden cage within turned slowly. Faster and faster it spun, faster and faster. Our thirty-eight uncapped combs blurred as the big cage gathered speed. Thirty-eight basswood frames merged into a single bright basswood wheel.

Lucy's hand crept into mine. This was our reward for a winter of labour with hammers and nails and paint brushes, assembling bee hives and frames. This was the aftermath of that springtime night of horror when we hived our packaged bees. This was the fine fruit of a summer spent dancing attendance upon a demanding, never satisfied horde of stinging insects. This was it, we told ourselves, as with unbelieving eyes we watched the honey —our honey—spatter in a golden rain on to the extractor walls.

We watched the bright flood cover the extractor bottom. We watched it flow to the pipe hole, and there sink in a miniature whirlpool as the pull of the power-driven honey pump caught it and sucked it away. We turned to the discharge end of the pump line, where it poked its nose down through the whitewashed ceiling into the open top of the strainer tank. Honey gurgled and bubbled downward in a tawny stream.

We turned flashlights on the lazy flood, and exclaimed at the glorious colour of it. We watched it fill the strainer tank, working its way through a set of four close-meshed monel metal screens. We watched it overflow the strainer, and discharge through a larger pipe, down past dull bronze valves into a shining storage vat. We watched our honey crawl and rise up the vat's bright sides.

Lucy and I stared like two bespectacled gollywogs in a trance. We had done it. Our management had produced it. Our honey house set-up was handling it. We could hardly believe it, but there it was, flooding down through the open valves, rising before our eyes in a golden flood that was topped with silver foam. It seemed a shame, so beautiful and fragrant it was, to even think of selling it.

"I do believe," I told Lucy, as we hung together over the vat side, "that there is more sheer beauty in a spoonful of honey than there is in a whole anthology of poetry."

"There is the whole story of a Medonte summer in ours," she agreed, "not to mention the fact that every single spoonful of it represents the life work of a bee."

"Not to mention that to gather a pound of it, our bees have flown the equivalent of twice around the world at the equator," I added.

"Not to mention," finished Lucy, in a wee small voice, "that one of your blistering, world-circling poets is crawling on my bare leg."

The world was a perfect place to us that night when, long after midnight, we crawled into bed to dream of great, white beeswax mountains, and glacial streams of nectar. We had close to a thousand pounds of honey in our vats, and there were many hundreds of fat combs still in the supers, awaiting our uncapping plane. To-morrow was another day. We would fill all our vats, and all our honey pails. If only there were a few less bees in the honey house . . . But what were a few bees?

A few bees! We went back into the honey house in the morning to find that the bees had taken over. Where the uncapping box had been was a crawling mound of bees. The extractor was lined with them. They were drowning by the thousands in the storage vat. The floor where honey had been spilled, was carpeted with them. The piled-up supers of extracted comb, was a howling inferno of them. They clouded the windows. They spotted the walls. They were everywhere, and they were still coming. They were after the honey—their honey. They were sucking it up through tens of thousands of sharp bee lips, toting it back to the bee-yard, and the hives that we had taken it from.

"What will we do?" shouted Lucy above the din of their roaring.

I didn't know. I ran about the honey house like a hen in a fit, tightening lids here, covering things there, fastening down this, blanketing that. I lit my smoker and filled the honey house with a dense cloud of smoke. I thought to drive the bees out. I didn't. I drove myself out. I stood in the workyard coughing and rubbing my eyes, praying for an inspiration, an idea, a plan of attack. Bees continued to pour into the honey house. Judging from the smoke that poured out of the cracks in it, the place was about as bee-tight as a rail fence.

"Do something!" yelled Lucy. "Swat 'em! Kick 'em! Don't stand there like a cigar store Indian."

A light lit in my smoke soaked head. I had a plan. My plan was to drag all the honey smeared supers of extracted comb out of the honey house, and set them up on a hillock about a hundred feet distant from it. My hope was that the bees, discouraged by the smoke in the honey house, would abandon it for this easier source of booty on the side hill. My fear was that they would merely call up reinforcements and work both honey house and supers.

We had to take that chance. Lucy and I waded through the smoke in the honey house like divers working on a muddy lake bottom, dragging the supers from it to the hillside. As the pile on the hillside grew, the bees found it, and soon we found ourselves more like divers than ever, plunging from a mixture of bees and smoke in the honey house, to a murk of undiluted bees on the hill. We shifted the last super, wiped our honey-wet hands on our honey-wet slacks, and ran honey-wet fingers through our honey-wet hair.

There was nothing more we could do except wait. We had made our honey house as bee-tight as we could. We had covered our extracted honey, and extracting equipment, as well as we could. We had baited our diversion as thoroughly as we could. We sat on the hillside thinking of the carpenter who had assured us that our honey house was so bee-tight that not even the ghost of a bee would be able to find its way into it. And we decided there and then that we would do the rest of our extracting in the dead of night, when no bee flies, and when only harmless wolves, and bats, and wildcats roam abroad.

# 30

## We Buy More Land

I SUPPOSE THAT IT WAS INEVITABLE THAT LUCY AND I, with over a ton of fine white honey in our storage vats, should look at our bee-yard and decide that forty-five hives were not enough. We wanted more hives, a hundred more hives. We saw no reason why we shouldn't eventually have five hundred, or even two thousand hives, scattered in little outyards all over the township.

"We'll be the bee kings of Medonte," I told Lucy, and waxed eloquent in a description of the new honey house we would have to build, with at least a half-a-dozen extractors set in line, and a long bank of tremendous storage tanks, "big enough to drown a club woman, or a cow in."

It was a nice dream, but just a dream. After a quick look at our bank books we decided that maybe, under the circumstances, we might satisfy ourselves with an increase of a mere fifty hives, for the time being. Even this small increase would, we knew, involve us once again in a winter-long orgy of work. Once again every available corner of the Owl Pen would fill with hive covers, and hive bodies, and hive bottoms, and hive stands. Once again we would have to burn our lamps at midnight making thousands of hive frames fitting them with wire, and sheets of beeswax.

But that worry was for the future. Our present chore was to find an outyard to hold our increase, for there was no room for it at Owl Pen. Our home yard was full. We borrowed a car, and once again roamed the township. We wanted one acre of land, situated in an area where there

were many blossoms, of the right sort, and no other bee-
yards. There had to be shade on the place, either second
growth bush, or an old orchard, and there had to be fresh
running water close at hand. The site had to be well
drained, and sheltered from north and northwest winds.

The hunt was splendid fun. Medonte, with its ten thousand hills, its tiny woodlands, and its old rail fences, is
like nothing on earth so much as a rich and ancient tapestry
unrolled for inspecting gods. We drove our little car down
coloured concession lines that might well have been lifted
straight from the centre of a mediaeval arras. Beauty
was our pied piper, and we came upon her, the wanton,
at every turn in the road.

We didn't care how many days, or weeks it took us
to find our outyard. We had plenty of time. There was
no hurry. Why should there be when all the world was
rich with sunshine and flowers? We stopped by the old
mill at Coulson, and went in among the cobwebs and the
meal sacks, for wheat, oats, and barley for our hens. The
miller took time off to tell us, after we had told him what
we were seeking in the way of land, as well as grain, that
on the hillside just above the mill, and overlooking the
millpond, was a bit of land that might suit.

"Years ago folks dreamed that there might be a big
town here," he explained. "The land was surveyed as a
town site. The bit I'm telling you about was cut off from
my dad's farm for building lots."

Lucy and I did not bother to go up the hill and look
at the land. The miller's description was enough for us.
It would do. We went seeking the owner, a farmer who
we were told lived just across the road from a red brick
church near a village some three miles distant. We turned
right, and we turned left. We drove up hill, and down
dale. We saw no village. We saw no church.

"We're lost," I told Lucy.

"Let's ask that farmer with the hay rack where we are," suggested Lucy, pointing ahead at an approaching team.

"Hey," I hailed the farmer.

"Yeh?" he pulled up his horses.

"I'm looking for a village named Hobart," I told him.

"This is it," he grinned, waving his hand at the rail fences and the grain fields. There were no houses.

"I'm looking for a red brick church," I continued.

"One hundred yards ahead," he grinned again.

"There's a farmer living across the road from it."

"I'm him," said the farmer with the rack.

I got out of the car and stood among the goldenrod at the side of the road. This was going to be difficult, I told myself. I don't like bargaining, and bargaining, it seems, is an inseparable part of every country transaction. Two girls in overalls, lying in the rack, each armed with a pitch fork, smiled shyly. I smiled back. The sun shone.

"I want to buy that land of yours at Coulson," I told the farmer, and grinned again at the two blue-denimed nymphs in the rack back of him.

"Sure," he said, "fifty dollars."

"Forty dollars," I countered, hardly able to believe my ears.

"Sold," said he.

I got out my pen, and my cheque book, and there by the side of the road, with the two grinning girls for witnesses, made the land ours. A green grasshopper walked across the face of my cheque book as I wrote. Birds sang as I passed the still wet slip of paper to the bearded farmer. He clamped it between his knees, and picked up the reins.

"Whoa, Ned," he said. "Whoa, Bess," and then, "the lilacs you'll find growing on that land was put there nearly a hundred years ago by the first of my tribe in these parts." He paused, "I hope you won't feel obliged to cut them all down."

I promised that I would not, and went back to the car.
Lucy had moved over into the driver's seat, and was waiting impatiently. We had wanted land. We had bought
land. It seemed reasonable to her that we should now
go back to Coulson and find out exactly what it was for
which we had paid our money.

"It's ours," she said, "we might as well look at it—that
is, if you have grinned enough at those two wenches on
the hay rack."

So back to Coulson we went, past the old gray mill,
past the broad mill pond, with its mighty willow trees,
its rushes and its ducks, and up the long hillside to the
place where the lilacs grew. We got out of our car, and
clambered through a gap in what was left of a fence. We
pushed our way through the lilacs and found ourselves
in a sun-flecked glade of second-growth poplar and wild
cherry trees. Beside us was an oblong depression in the
ground, some rubble, and a row of stones. A pioneer
home had stood there. A pioneer wife had planted the
lilacs we had waded through. Ahead of us were ancient
apple trees, gnarled and broken now, and close to death.
A pioneer had loved fruit. Huge elms marked the corners
of our purchase. The land was level and well drained,
exactly what we wanted, exactly what we had been looking for, exactly what our first outyard should be.

# PART 11

## Imperfect Peace

Our Plesance here is all vain glory,
This fals world is but transitory,
The flesh is bruckle, the Feynd is slee:—

*Timor Mortis Conturbat Me.*

WILLIAM DUNBAR, 1465

# 𝟛𝟙

## *We Come Down to Earth*

SOONER OR LATER, EVERYONE WHO LIVES ON A CONCESSION
line learns that to walk on air in the country is to come to
earth with a bump. Lucy and I learned. We walked on
air for days and weeks after the completion of our white
honey harvest. Then came Nemesis. One lovely morning
we got up with the sun. We walked through sunshine
and lark song uphill to our chicken house. We opened
our chicken house door. Our eyes bulged in utter unbelief
at what we saw. We bumped.

Two buxom pullets lay sprawled in death on the floor
at our feet. Over two thirds of our fine young flock of
yesterday stood huddled about in the litter, with drooping
wings, and closed eyes, and a strange new puffiness of
breast. The feed troughs were untouched. The water

pans were empty. The few healthy birds that remained seemed filled with a fiendish desire to tear their ailing sisters apart. The air was filled with feathers, shrieks and groans. It was not pleasant being in our chicken house that day.

Lucy turned with a drawn face back to the goat pen, and the milking. I picked up a dead chicken. It looked all right. There was no sign of disease. I fingered its body. It did not feel right. The crop was puffy like a half-inflated balloon, and empty except for a bit of water that gurgled and sploshed as I felt it through the bird's thin skin.

I picked up one of the ailing birds. The poor thing shook and shivered in my hands. Its crop too was puffy, and empty except for water. I picked up others. They were all the same. There was death in their eyes. As I stood there a bird by the water fountain lay down, kicked violently, stretched its neck, gasped, squawked twice, and was still, except for a spasmodic quivering of its feathers. I picked it up, and carried it out with the two other corpses, to the red wheel barrow in the yard.

What to do? I hadn't the foggiest idea. A small voice kept whispering that somehow the fault was mine. I had done something that I ought not to have done, or left undone that which was essential to the well-being of our fowl. But what? But what? I couldn't guess. No chicks in the township had been babied and coddled as ours had. No chicks had been fed as extravagantly as ours. None were better housed or more cleanly kept.

I went back to the Owl Pen with a dead bird in my hand, laid it on the living room table, and spread my poultry books around it. They told me nothing. Nothing that I read in them of the various ills that afflict chickdom fitted what I had seen in our laying house, or with what lay on the table in front of me. There was a chance that a post mortem might tell me something. The books advised such examination. I determined to play pathologist.

It was with some trepidation that I took a sharp knife out of the kitchen and began my task. All I knew about the innards of a chicken was that certain of them properly cooked and spiced, made good gravy. But it was not as a cook, or as a lover of good food that I looked at them now. I spread them out, all the little pipes, and valves, and pumps and strainers that fill a chicken, and went over them, one by one. They held the secret to what was wrong with my flock, and had I the brains to read them right, the reason and the cure. It was a mucky job.

Fortunately, the message in the innards was, to use an older English, writ plain as a pike staff. Even I could read it. The gizzard was stuffed with shavings—hard packed —stone-like shavings from our chicken house floor. Our birds had been eating their litter, stuffing themselves with it, eating themselves to death with it. That was my diagnosis.

I turned to my books again. They all agreed that in the case of an impacted crop the thing to do was to operate, open it up with a pair of scissors, empty it, and sew it up again with a needle and thread, just as one would sew up a hole in an old glove. They did not say what to do when the impaction was in the gizzard. Certainly surgery on such a deeply buried organ was, even if possible to experts, beyond my skill. I pictured myself in a feather-littered, squawk-filled chicken house, digging with a sharp knife into the gizzards of a hundred struggling birds. The thought curled my few remaining hairs.

But something had to be done. I cudgled my brains. I had to save our flock. There was a way if I could only find it. Somehow, as I searched frantically in the back corners of my brain for a solution to my problem, I remembered words spoken by Joe Johnston, years ago in talking about the scientific feeding of pigs.

"My pigs ain't scientific," said Joe, "I don't feed 'em scientific. Science would kill 'em. I just figger out what I would like if I was a pig. I just reckon up what would be good for me if I walked on all fours in a pen. I give 'em that. They do good on it."

What would I do if I had a gizzard, if my gizzard was stuffed to a stone-like hardness with wood shavings? What had my mother given me, donkey's years ago, when I ate the stuffings out of a doll? I went upstairs to the medicine cabinet. Epsom salts were there. Castor oil was there. As I read the labels on the packages I did not have to shut my eyes to see myself, thirty-five years ago, kicking and yelling in my father's arms, while my mother held my nose and poured the vile stuff into me. I took the packages out of the cabinet and went back up the hill to the chicken house.

"It's kill or cure," I told Lucy. "Kill, and we'll be no worse off than if we do nothing. Cure, and we'll know what to do the next time."

Lucy and I spent the rest of the morning in the chicken house, she with a bottle of castor oil in one hand, and a silver teaspoon in the other, I with a tin bucket between my knees, and one or another of our hundred ailing birds in my arms. One after another we picked them up and held them head down over the bucket, and massaged their swollen crops, emptying them of the sour water and foul smelling gas that filled them. One after another we took them by their trembling heads, forced open their beaks and dosed them with castor oil, one full teaspoonful to each bird. We stood up from our task at last, oil soaked and water soaked, scratched, feather-flecked, and pecked. We swept the shavings from the chicken house floor, and put down a thick covering of fresh straw. We filled the water pans with an almost saturated solution of Epsom salts, filled the feed troughs with fresh mash, and went out into the sunlight. We had either killed or cured our flock. We didn't know which. Time would tell.

All day long our pullets crowded the water fountains. They ignored their food. All night long they huddled in miserable, trembling clusters on the straw covered floor. They ignored their roosts. In the morning we found three more of them dead. The living were still sad-eyed and unhappy. The next day we picked another three corpses out of the litter. The third day we found two more dead, and watched two more die. It seemed to us that it was merely a matter of time before they all found their way into the red wheel barrow, and so into a hole in the flower garden.

"They might as well die in the sunshine," sighed Lucy. "Let's let them out."

We opened the bolt holes in the chicken house wall and let our flock out into the runs. Dirty, bedraggled, and oil-stained, our pullets wandered listlessly among the grasses and wild flowers on the hillside. We looked at them without hope, noticing that most of our pets, birds that we had named, were among the missing. Bubbles Eyes was gone, and so was Kiss Me Quick, and Lady Bess. Paunchy was gone, and Toeless and Cuddlesome. Of all our particular friends, there remained only one, poor Dirty Back, and she wobbled weakly as she walked.

Thank whatever gods may be for roosters. I think it was our cockerels, rather than our castor oil and Epsom salts, that saved our flock for us. The second day after we had let our flock out into the runs, they began to eye the cockerels that crowded the hillside on the far side of the wire. They began to preen a little. They say that when a woman begins to worry about her appearance, and struggles to put on a bit of lip rouge before the doctor arrives, the crisis is past. That is the way it was with our pullets. They began pacing the fence line, seeking a way to their boy friends. Two of them finally flew the fence and decamped with two of our cockerels into an adjoining hay field. Three cockerels found their way over the fence into the yard with the pullets. That did it. Lucy and I stopped worrying and ordered another half ton of chicken feed.

## 32

### We Don't Like Honey

To walk on air and then bump is one thing. To bump and bounce, and bump again is another. Of course Lucy and I had heard of the old superstition that troubles never come singly, that they come in threes, but we were not impressed. We put that yarn down as an old wives' tale, something to be tucked away in a scarecrow's hat with the old belief that one should never plant seeds during the waning of the moon, or begin a new job or work in a new field at the end of the week.

We saw nothing ominous in the little groups of exploring bees that hung all day long outside the screened windows of our living room, that buzzed by the honey house door, that crawled along the cracks at the backs of the hives in the bee-yard. We gave no thought at all to the small but growing mounds of dead bees that lay in the grass at the foot of the alighting board in front of nearly every hive. We were too busy dreaming of the amber flood of autumn honey so soon, we were sure, to be ours.

Orders poured in on us. We accepted money from innocent housewives and trusting strangers, and saw wealth grow in a neat clinking pile in the bottom of the butter crock in the kitchen. Anticipating the moment when our autumn crop of honey would be harvested and delivered, and this money actually ours, we ordered a paint spraying machine, and made inquiries about an expensive, registered nanny goat. I bought a camera. Lucy looked at the latest thing in frocks.

"There is an awful cloud of bees hanging over one of the hives," said Lucy, coming into the work shop where I was busy making a burglar alarm for the chicken house.

"A play fight," I said, and went on with my work.

"You'd better take a look," said Lucy, coming back an hour later, with a worried look on her face. "Something funny is going on in that yard. There are bees all over the place . . . millions of them."

With a sinking feeling in the pit of my stomach, I put down my plane. Words read weeks earlier in a bee book, and having to do with the robbing that is likely to start during a break in a honey flow, came to my mind. Robbing! That was it! I went into the bee yard.

The "awful cloud" that Lucy had reported seeing over one of the hives was still there. Bees by the tens of thousands were racing in and out of a wide gap left in the top of the hive by a warped cover. I lifted it off. A new cloud rose in my face. I picked out one of the combs. It had been chewed to pieces. There was no honey left in it. I lifted off the super, and went down into the hive body. Every comb in it had been riddled. The honey was gone. The defending inhabitants were dead, their torn and crumpled bodies strewn on the hive floor, and in a heap at the hive entrance. Carnage and destruction! The invaders had done their job well. There was nothing to salvage, nothing to save.

I hurried from hive to hive. At every entrance robbers were hovering. At every entrance there was fighting, wtih hundreds of bees locked in mortal combat. At every entrance there was a tremendous pile of dead. Dead bees were everywhere, on the hive tops, in the grass, on the gravel path. I contracted every entrance, leaving only a small hole that would admit a few bees at a time, so giving the inhabitants a better chance to defend their homes and stores.

I then went a second time around the bee-yard, this time with big handfuls of wet grass, which I threw down in front of each hive, blocking and veiling the contracted entrances, making it still harder for the would-be invaders to force a way in, making it still easier for the inhabitants to organize an adequate defence. That was the theory of it. That, the books said, was the thing to do when robbing got out of hand.

The invaders still came on, worming their way into the mounds of wet grass, filling them so that the grass moved and heaved, as though alive. I got a watering can, and wet the grass again, this time with a mixture of carbolic acid and water. The bees in the grass, defenders and invaders alike, died when the acid hit them. Other battalions, both from within the hives and from the bee-filled air above, took their places, and they died too. I tried smoke. The fighting lessened not a bit.

"What's the verdict?" shouted Lucy from the hillside.

"We're finished," I told her. "The Owl Pen bee-yard is caput."

The next morning it was quieter in the bee-yard. There was a measure of peace in it, a certain uneasy stillness. I went about the hives. There was at least a pint and a half of dead bees at the foot of every alighting board. In front of some hives there was more—a blackening pile of crumpled bodies mixed with crumbs of wax, and cell-shaped pellets of jade-green, and yellow, and bright red pollen. I did not need to lift the hive covers to know the story. More colonies had died. More defenders had been overwhelmeed. More comb had been gutted. More brood had been killed. I counted them. Three more. A total of four destroyed entirely, I dared not even guess at the number that had been weakened by the fray to the point where they could not hope to survive the winter.

Some days later, there having been no further outbreaks

of robbing, I felt that it was safe to open a few of the hives. I wanted to know what honey there was in them. It was time to take off the autumn crop, and time to plan for winter feeding. I wanted to know why my bees, the gentle little honey gatherers of the summer months, had so suddenly changed into murderous, rampaging fiends.

I was not long in finding out. There was practically no honey at all in any of the hives in the yard. The fall flow had been a complete failure. The blaze of autumn beauty all around, the goldenrod and the asters, had fed our eyes and starved our bees. Only the thirty-five pounds of light honey that we had left on each hive when taking off the summer crop had kept them alive. And most of it was gone. No wonder our bees had turned pirate.

That afternoon we took every super off every hive, and moved them all into the honey house. There was a little honey in the combs, a half pound here, three pounds there, a mere drop in the bucket of our bees' winter needs. We extracted it, and it just three-quarters filled the strainer tank.

"Our feeder trays will be here in a few days' time," I told Lucy. "When they come, we'll feed all this back to the bees, so much to each hive, share and share alike."

Had we known then what we know now, we would not have waited for the arrival of our feeders. We would have fed the honey into the hives by the spoonful, if necessary. We would have held our bees' noses, one at a time, the whole two millions of them and poured the stuff, willy-nilly down their blasted little throats. But we did not know. We did not even suspect until our feeder trays arrived, days late, and we prepared to return our pittance of autumn honey to our hungry bees.

"Here goes," said Lucy, and hung a bucket under the spout of the honey gate. She pulled open the cock. No honey poured into her bucket. No thick brown flood welled out. "We've been robbed!" she wailed.

She was wrong, unfortunately wrong. The honey was still in the strainer, granulated, set, congealed into an almost cement-like mass around the five fine monel metal screens that fill the gadget. We shook the tank. We kicked it. We poked at it with sticks. For the rest of the day we worked at that congealed fiend of a tank. We set a ring of electric heaters around it. We poured boiling water over it. We sprayed it with live steam. We ran red-hot pokers into it. At midnight we quit.

The next morning we recast our plan of attack. We decided we would do nothing with the strainer during the day. We would simply surround it with heat, all the heat that we could muster, and let nature take its course. Surely, we told ourselves, after a full twenty-four hours of stewing in its own juice, it would give up at least part of its petrified load. Surely, it would then be a simple matter to run the honey off into our pails, distribute it among the hives, and have done with the job.

So it might have been. But a storm blew up, and the power went off, and the strainer tank chilled, and the half melted honey in it stayed half melted—an exasperating cross between pig lead and asphalt. We loaded the awful thing on to our red wheel barrow, and lugged it up to the Owl Pen, to the wood stove in the Owl Pen kitchen. We built a hot fire under it, and then we rushed it with pincers and wrecking bars and screw drivers.

By sheer main force, but with due respect for the expensiveness of the gadget, we tore it apart. We clawed at its vitals. We heaved, and grunted, and drew the nested, honey-cemented screens out of its bowels. We spread them all over the kitchen. We wallowed in honey. Honey spread out of the kitchen into the living room, up the stairs into the bedroom, out of the bedroom into the bathroom.

"I hate honey," said Lucy, "honey is bunk."

We fed our bees. We cleaned up the mess we had made in the Owl Pen, and then we took our treasure trove out of the old butter crock. We tucked it into a score of white envelopes addressed to the friends and neighbours, and trusting strangers who had ordered fall honey from us. All we had the heart to say by way of explanation was:

"Sorry, we have no fall honey for sale."

## 33

### *We Welcome Trouble*

LUCY AND I ADMITTED TO OURSELVES, AND OUR NEIGHBOURS, that there might be, after all, something in the old belief that troubles never come singly. We had almost lost our flock of Chanticler pullets. Our autumn honey crop had been a failure. According to the old belief, one more disaster, or near disaster, was to be inflicted upon us. We wondered what next would happen.

"You don't need to wonder," comforted a farming friend. "Just be patient. Wait and see."

We hadn't long to wait. Trouble came to us on wings, in the shape of a dapper little gentleman in a gray suit, a claret coloured waistcoat, a bottle green hat, and orange-red shoes—a wild mallard drake, no less. Trouble came to us out of the blue, at the quacked invitation of our own tame ducks. We found it when we went to gather the eggs, taking an afternoon snack with our Rouens out of the big trough by the goat pen door.

Lucy and I were halfway up the side hill pasture field, halfway from the Owl Pen to the strutting and gossiping little group of ducks, geese, and cockerels by the goat house door, when we first caught sight of the stranger. He hurtled skyward, a flying gem that glistened and shone in the bright sunlight.

"Look!" I shouted. "One of our ducks is flying away!"

"Nonsense," said the mistress of Owl Pen. "It's a wild duck come visiting. We're breaking up a tea party."

The lovely stranger circled low, between us and the sun. Our ducks quacked up to him, urging him to return, insisting,

we had no doubt, that he would come to no harm, telling
him that there was more mash in the trough. The wildling
quacked down to them, telling them, we guessed, certain
recent experiences he had had with humans in weedy
Matchedash Bay. He quacked and circled. Our birds
swiveled their heads, as we swiveled ours, tracking him
through the cloud-flecked sky.

A message of sorts must have passed between the tame
ducks on the ground, and the wild one in the sky, for our
ducks did suddenly a most unheard-of-thing. They turned
their fat backs on the still half-filled feed trough, and
made a bee-line for the pond. They waddled and rolled
across the pasture field, tumbled down the pond bank,
and splashed into the water. The stranger quacked twice
more, circled the Owl Pen once more, and then splashed
down beside them.

"Come away," I told Lucy, "come away quietly. Let
the chickens wait for their feed. Let the goats wait for
their milking. Let everything wait. If we keep out of the
way, and do not disturb that little stranger, he may stay
with our ducks. He may follow them into their sleeping
pen. If he does, we'll have him. We'll make him a part
of the Owl Pen. We'll add him to our flock."

Trouble, we know now, was being welcomed to Owl
Pen. With elaborate stealth, and by roundabout route that
kept rods between us and Moonstone Creek, we made our
way back to the house. We set our still-filled food baskets
on the living room floor, and put our still-empty egg
baskets beside them. We dashed for the bedroom window,
and the view that it commanded of the pond and creek.
We bent our noses sideways against the window pane.

The stranger was still on the water, bobbing and gossiping with his hosts. Had we guessed what he was saying,
had we known him for what he was, we would have taken
a rifle down from the wall and blasted him into whatever

valhalla ducks go to when they die. We would have shushed him off the Owl Pen Pond. We would have rubbed him out. But we didn't know. We gabbled our admiration of him and sighed our hopes that he would stay.

Certainly, he was something to admire. Our pond that afternoon was a living tapestry, richly illustrative of what man can do when he turns his mind from the silliness of politics and trade, and dabbles like a lesser god in the living flesh and future of living things. As Lucy and I stood at our bedroom window, there passed in review before us the three massive exhibition-type Rouen ducks that we had lately secured from a famous breeder at Vankleek Hill. Behind these giants sailed our own five Owl Pen Rouens, smaller more spritely birds, without the pendulous dewlaps and low slung keels of the show birds. Behind these again bobbed our own three domesticated mallards. And in and out, among and between them all, sailed our little wild mallard visitor, a brightly-coloured mite weighing no more than a pound and a half—a mighty atom indeed.

The magic of the spectacle, for Lucy and I, lay in the fact that the little wildling represented the seed from which all the other ducks had sprung. He was what our domesticated mallards had been half a dozen generations ago. He was what the great-great-grandfathers, a hundred times removed, of our mighty show birds had been. The little wild drake was an exact miniature of the larger birds, feather for feather, and hue for hue. He differed from them in no way except size. He was a living portrait of the father of them all.

"It's almost ridiculous," I whispered.

"It's sweet," said Lucy.

We took our numbed noses from the window pane, and had tea. We bent them again to the glass when tea was done. The hours crept by. The sun changed into a big

red pumpkin and crawled down the western sky. The
shadows deepened, spread, and engulfed the pond. Our
ducks, and their tiny guest, still bobbed on the waters.

"They'll be going to bed soon now," I murmured.

"You hope," said Lucy.

"They always do at this time," I insisted.

We fingered our aching noses and waited. The last
light left the hills. Stars twinkled wanly overhead. A new
moon rode like a silver schooner in a ghostly sea of clouds.
The pond gleamed darkly. We could hear our ducks.
Sometimes we could just see them, wee cavorting silhouettes
against a moonbeam on the water.

"Remember seeing them like that once before?" asked
Lucy with a wide malicious grin.

I did. All thoughts of the little wild drake flew out of
my head. Was history repeating itself? Were our ducks
again intending to spend the night on the pond? The last
time they had attempted such folly I had gone in swimming after them, and had driven them from the water
into their sleeping pen. That foray had cost me a good
pair of socks and a bloody toe.

"That water was warm then," said Lucy. "Now it is
cold, very cold."

"I know it," I gritted unhappily.

That blasted wildling! It had talked our ducks into
folly. That was what they had been gabbling about on
the pond. Our ducks had been good ducks. Not once since
that historic night when I went swimming after them had
they even attempted to break the Owl Pen law and spend
a night on the water. Night after night, week after week,
month after month, they had waddled at twilight up the
bank to their sleeping pen, to spend the hours of darkness
indoors, as all decent ducks should. Now a rank outsider,
an unpedigreed creature of the swamps had put ideas
into their heads. My lips pursed in a very reasonable fac-

simile of a fox's jaws as I thought of him, whispering and gugging there in the darkness, leading our ducks astray, and leading me, as surely as though I had a ring in my nose, straight down out of Owl Pen into the cold, black water of the Moonstone.

With the forlorn hope that our turncoat quackers might have a spark of decency left in their multi-coloured carcasses, I carried a flashlight to the pondside. Ducks do not like lights at night. Ordinarily, they can be driven with a beam of light as surely and easily as one can drive cattle with a switch. Had it not been for that trouble-making stranger I might have driven them, by flashlight, down the creek, across the pond, up the bank to their pens.

But with him at their head, driving was impossible. When I turned on the light, he panicked and they panicked after him. The whole flock raced around the pond in a wild melee of frantically paddling feet, thrashing wings and gaping bills. Our birds turned and twisted as the light hit them. They dived. They quacked and gasped. They went completely mad. And always at their head, leading them in their headlong, crazy flight was that blasted wildling, that pretty little wild mallard drake that had flown in to tea.

Once again the choice was mine. I could go back into the house, and leave my truant quackers to the tender mercies of the night, and the teeth of the night, or I could once again go in after them. I stood thinking it over. Never had the pond looked so big, or black, or so cold. As Lucy came to the water's edge with a second light I waded in. The water was cold!

"Did you hurt yourself?" she shouted, as the water crept over my knees.

"No," I quavered.

"Then what are you groaning about?" she wanted to know.

I didn't answer her. I couldn't. The water was already up to my waist, filling my trousers with unmentionable horrors, and my mind with unmentionable fears. The ducks panicked again. I stumbled after them. The water rose to my arm pits. A wet duck hit me in the face.

"Your moaning gives me the willies," said Lucy.

I attempted a bitter, sarcastic laugh.

I think I quacked.

Our ducks weren't long leaving the pond. I was hardly into the water than they were out of it, waddling frantically up the bank, quacking wildly through the long grasses and dried aster stalks, tumbling headlong into their pen. We counted them. Three—six—nine—eleven—all were accounted for—all except the wild mallard drake, the cause of all our trouble. We turned our lights on the pond again. He was still there, twisting, flapping, diving, racing to escape he knew not what.

"He is pretty," said Lucy.

My chattering teeth mangled the profanity of my reply.

# PART 12

## Autumn Glory

*O Western wind, when wilt thou blow,*
*That the small rain down can rain?*
*Christ, that my love were in my arms*
*And I in my bed again!*

ANON.

# 34

## *We Contemplate Death*

TIME RAN. IT SEEMED TO LUCY AND ME THAT WE HAD barely finished wiping the mud of spring from our boots, and the sweat of summer from our necks, than autumn was piling coloured leaves about our door. The glory was already going from the maple trees. Yellowish birch leaves spattered the hurrying waters of Moonstone Creek. We prepared for winter.

Clanking trucks wheeled into the Owl Pen workyard, leaning and lurching with their loads of rough-barked wood. Our house was small, but to cook our meals and warm our bones through the long white months to come we needed a pile of wood four feet wide, four feet high, and ninety-six feet long. This had to be cut fine, and short, for the kitchen stove, and into heavy, two-foot billets for the fire-place.

It was a man's job. Well, I had done it before. I reached for my axe and felt weak. I felt ill.

The laziness of the season for autumn, despite the work that is done in it is a lazy time of year, got into my blood. I lay in bed with a thermometer stuck in my mouth, with a temperature of 101, a pile of books, a plate of apples, and a pipeful of tobacco. According to the experts, I had influenza. According to my way of looking at it, I was having a lucky break. There were twelve huge cords of wood to split and pile, and I could neither split nor pile them. There was half a ton of sugar to bed to the bees, and I couldn't feed it. I reached for an apple (groan), and turned the pages of a favourite book (groan), and felt sorry for the people who were feeling sorry for me.

It was fun lying in bed, looking out of the bedroom window into the workyard, where hired men were splitting and piling our winter's supply of wood, or into the bee-yard where another minion was waddling between the hives with full buckets of sugar syrup, filling the feeder trays, feeding the bees. Of course, I had to pretend to loathe it. I told Lucy it was unfair to saddle her with the chores as well as the housework. I insisted on getting up. I argued that getting up for just a little while and doing a bit of the lighter work would not hurt me at all. For one heart-stopping moment I thought she was going to agree with me. She didn't. With an inward groan of relief I heard her say that I simply must stay in bed until my temperature went down to normal. I asked, somewhat weakly, for another glass of apple juice, and another piece of cake.

The next day, I really did feel ill. I had felt fine in the morning and as restless as usual, but as the day grew towards noon I began to sweat. Streams of perspiration ran down my forehead into my eyes. My pyjamas grew damp, and then wet. I could actually feel my temperature going

up, and up, and up. I gasped for breath. I put down my
book and turned my face to the wall.

As I lay there feeling very sorry for myself, some of my
grandmother's sickroom wisdom came to my mind. I remembered how she had always impressed it upon my
mother, when I was a lad, that under no circumstances
should a person ill in bed and with a temperature, be
allowed to cool off. The more he sweated, the more
blankets and comforters should be piled over him. A chill
was the thing to avoid. A sweater over his pyjamas was a
good thing, and a sock, especially a well-worn dirty sock,
around his neck helped, too.

Lucy was below helping our visiting bee-master mix
the syrup for the feeder trays. I did not want to disturb
her. I staggered out of bed and across the room to the
clothes closet. I got a heavy sweater and put it on. I
went then to the linen closet and got a heavy blanket and
an eiderdown comforter. Back to bed I went, and spread
these coverings over me. The journey had cooled my
wet pyjamas. I shivered. Maybe I was getting a chill.
I took my dressing gown from the foot of the bed and
spread it over the eiderdown.

"No use worrying," I told myself. "No use at all."

I took up my book again, and tried to read. I couldn't.
Beads of perspiration ran into my eyes. It stung. Drops
of the stuff rolled down on the page. It was a good book.
I didn't want to soil it. I put it down, and turned my
head wearily to the wall again. I felt dizzy. I was burning up. The room blurred. I slept.

I don't know how long I slept. An hour maybe, no
more. I awoke to find Lucy standing at the foot of the
bed with a glass of apple juice in her hand and a look of
utter bewilderment on her face. I reached a wet hand
for the glass.

"Thank you, dear," I whispered.

"Do you mind telling me what damned foolishness you're up to now?" she demanded, drawing the glass back just out of my reach.

"Please, darling," I quavered. "I'm ill."

Lucy put the glass of apple juice down on the dressing table. Then she yanked my dressing gown off the eiderdown. She yanked the eiderdown off the blanket. She yanked the blanket off the cotton coverlet that was below it. She turned the coverlet down, pulled me into a sitting position, and slid the sweater up over my shoulders, over my head—off. She even took my well-worn sock away. She opened the window.

"Darling," I protested.

"You idiot," she stormed.

"But I have a temperature . . . "

"Of course you have a temperature," she shouted, and subsided into a chair, shouting with laughter.

I didn't understand. It seemed cruel of her, and not at all like her. Usually Lucy was most sympathetic. Now, with me lying in front of her, at death's door for all she knew, she was laughing at me, laughing in my face.

"I thought you loved me," I whispered.

Lucy whooped again with laughter, horrible, unfeeling laughter. I turned my face to the wall. I heard her cross the room and stand by the bedside.

"All afternoon," she said, "all day, for that matter, while you have been lying up here in bed feeling sorry for yourself, I have been slaving in the kitchen boiling gallons and tens of gallons of water in order to make more sugar syrup for your nasty little bees. From early morning I have had a roaring fire in the cookstove, on a warm day like this. From early morning I have stood over a red-hot stove, in a cloud of steam cooking bee-food. All day long I have worried because the pipe from that stove runs up through the floor into this bedroom right beside your bed.

I knew that the heat and the steam were making the upstairs unbearably hot . . . "

Again the room rang with her laughter.

"I didn't know you were up here closing windows, putting on sweaters, and old socks, and eiderdowns, and blankets, and dressing gowns. No wonder you are hot. No wonder you think you have a temperature. No wonder you think you are dying."

I was glad that my face was turned to the wall.

# 35

## *We Do as We Would be Done By*

THERE IS IN MEDONTE A STRANGE MAGIC THAT SENDS A
man walking windy uplands in the autumn of the year,
to listen to the whisper and swish of wind in the pine
branches, to hear only the murmur of his own hay being
nuzzled by cattle in the byre at home. There is something in the air, or in the waters of Moonstone Creek that
sends a man along the hilltops, smelling the stars, and
thinking of home-made bread. Let an eagle scream in
his ears and he will think of the rusty hinges on the barnyard gate. Let a rainbow flare in his face and he will
think of his wife's flower garden.

That is the way it was with Lucy and me. When we
read in the newspapers of the big fair that was soon to
be held in the city, we thought only of Beefy, our pet
rooster, and how well he would look with a red ribbon
around his neck, and the name "Owl Pen" on his cage
tag. It must have been the air, or the water, or the magic
of the hills that made us dream so, for Beefy was by no
means the largest cockerel at Owl Pen, and there was
at least one black feather in his otherwise white coat.
He was not, to tell the horrid truth, all that a cockerel
of his breed should be.

But he was Beefy, our pal, and no ordinary bird.

No ordinary bird deserts its own kind entirely, to spend
every possible minute of every day at the heels of its
human owners. No ordinary bird eats meat, bread, and
potatoes in preference to poultry food, as Beefy did. As
time wore on Lucy and I became possessed of the weird

idea that our pet rooster did not know that he was a
rooster. He acted as though he suffered from the illusion
that he was himself a human being. He did our chores
with us. He helped us feed the ducks. He counted the
geese with us. He stood by while we milked the goats.
And he was always shouting at us to come and share his
latest find, an earthworm, or a wriggling slug.

Beefy absolutely refused to let us out of his sight. He
joined Lucy in the vegetable garden. He worked with
me in the bee-yard, and bore his stings more stoically
than I. He climbed ladders with us, and gave us the
benefit of his advice while we laid shingles. He dug
trenches with us, and though I once accidently laid him
him out cold with a shovel, refused to leave until the job
was done. He even, on more than one occasion, stood
approvingly by while we prepared one of his fellows for
Sunday dinner.

Beefy was quite a lad. Though he never attempted to
fight us, and even when we teased him offered us no more
in return than a bit of belligerent shadow boxing, he had
no liking for strangers. More than one woman visitor
left Owl Pen with the mark of his beak showing through
the silk on her legs. More than one small boy regretted
his temerity in provoking Beefy to attack. More than one
grown man had to fight him off with a stick. The world
to Beefy was a jungle, and all strangers were enemies.
He did his best to protect us, and though our friends cursed
him, we loved him for it.

We might have continued with our plan to send our
strange rooster to the fair if we had not chanced to look up
a book that told us what should be done to put a bird in
"prime showroom condition". That finished our dream,
and Beefy's chance for glory. Beefy stayed home. What
that book said we should do to our trusting rooster just to

make him look beautiful enough to satisfy an effete city
judge was utterly horrible.

Of course, it might be pointed out that what was ad-
vocated for our rooster was no worse than that which
fashionable women inflict upon themselves in their quest
for loveliness, but there is a difference. Women make
their own choice. As a matter of fact, some of them seem
actually to enjoy being soaked, scraped, slapped and massaged, painted and varnished. It is not necessary to grab
them by the legs and neck and truss them helplessly into
a hammock before beginning work on them. They seem
actually anxious to endure such treatment, willing to pay
for such mayhem and assault. But a chicken is different.
A chicken does have to be grabbed and trussed. A chicken
has dignity. A chicken objects. Chickens are sensitive.

Having grabbed our outraged rooster by the neck and
trussed him into a hammock with his two legs sticking
out through holes in the bottom, we were, according to
our book, ready to begin. We were, so to speak, to start
from the bottom and work up. Beefy's legs and feet were
to be made as lovely as those that Cleopatra toddled on
when she simpered in to wink at Anthony. We were to
wash our rooster's knobby props with mild soap and warm
rain water. We were to scrub them gently with a soft
brush. We were to anoint them with a fine lotion made
of pure alcohol and rectified olive oil. We were to smooth
them with pumice powder, trim them with nail scissors,
shape the cuticle at the ends of the claws and the scales
of the legs with an orange stick, and polish with a piece
of soft new chamois leather.

This was just the beginning. We had then, according
to our book, to make Beefy sweet all over. Having cleaned
and polished and prettied up his feet and legs, we had
now to give him a bath. This was to be no simple one-tub
sort of bath, the sort that might satisfy a queen-empress

or a duck. Our rooster was to be dunked into no fewer than three tubs, all filled with fresh rain water, all heated to exactly the right temperature, and all made nicely fluffy with rich soap suds. We were to take our Beefy by the scruff of the neck and hold him submerged in the first tub until all his feathers softened, and the loose dirt fell away. Then we were to lave him gently in the second tub, and rinse him in the third.

There remained, if our bird still lived, one more step in this process of avian beautification. We were to take Beefy out of his scented warm water inferno and drop him straight, ker-plunk, into a polar hell. We were to plunge him into a bucket of clean cold water, and hold him there for several minutes "to harden the bird and prevent it from catching cold". At this point the book advised that it was well to have handy a bottle of whiskey. If Beefy fainted, we were to pour the stuff, a spoonful at a time, down his poor limp, throat. Whiskey! Not even a cocktail! Just plain hootch!

That finished it. We closed the book and put it away on a shelf reserved for books that are seldom, if ever, read. We do not think that we will ever need that book again. Beefy and his sons and daughters, even unto the ultimate generation of chickens at Owl Pen are safe from fame, if this be the price of fame. Never will birds of ours go gadding into town with the smell of liquor on their breaths. Never will fowl of ours strut, or stagger, at the Royal Winter Fair. Well, not this year anyhow . . .

# 36

## *We Chore*

A SOLITARY FARMER AND A PLODDING TEAM, PLOUGHING THE
last furrow in a hillside field . . . the half-heard cry of a
girl on a distant farm calling cattle home . . . the bark of
a dog . . . the smell of woodsmoke . . . the whispered
laughter of Moonstone Creek . . . this was evening at
the Owl Pen in the autumn of the year, evening and
choring time.

Every day when the clock struck five, Lucy handed me
the feed buckets and the milk pail. I called the dog. We
put a screen in front of the fireplace to keep errant sparks
from our oiled floor, pulled on caps and jackets and headed
for the barn. Every day, just as the setting sun caught
like a big apple in the topmost branches of the elm on
the hill, we crossed the ragged Owl Pen lawn, passed the
dry well, and opened the pasture field gate.

Our welcome was always the same. Our ducks always
quacked impatiently demanding their evening meal. Our
geese were always defiant, following us with outstretched
necks and hissing beaks. Our chickens clucked and clattered. Our cockerels strutted and crowed. Always we
said "hello" to Beefy, our pet rooster, and to Dirty Back,
our pet hen, and always they said hello to us.

There was nothing particularly eventful in our choring
time. Chores are chores, even in Medonte, and even in
the autumn of the year. The days brought no changes,
except of sunshine and of rain. We liked it so. It was
always Thunder that yapped at our heels. It was always
Josephine and Suzanne our two goats that ba-ah'd us a

welcome as we opened the goat pen door. It was always Jo that we milked first, and always Sue that managed to steal a mouthful of wheat out of the grain bin. It was always, I do believe, the same chipmunk that Skudger, one of the Owl Pen cats, chased every day at choring time out from under the mash hopper in the yard.

We liked it that way. Change, for the sake of change, is not welcome on a farm. Change usually spells disaster, a sick animal, or a balky new one, a broken implement, or a lost tool. Change is something that forces a new rhythm into an old familiar pattern of work, so that a man is at sixes and sevens with himself and his work for days on end. On the farm old ways, known animals, and used tools are best. Ruts are comfortable things. They make for steady going and smooth sailing. They are a barnyard tradition. It is only a fool in the country who would hitch his wagon to a star. Lucy and I had found that out our own hard way.

But all this is not to suggest that we did not have our moments of romance and high adventure. We had them mixed with our chicken feed and goat fodder as part of our choring. We had them in the splendid beauty of an autumn storm that swept our valley from end to end in a flurry of coloured leaves. We had them, and we will remember them when we are grown old.

It was just an ordinary storm. It did no damage. It made no headlines in the newspapers. It left behind it no scars to tell a new day that our Medonte had lately been a battle ground for rampaging gods. Farmer Jim ploughed all through it, making the last field of Plum Tree Farm fit for seed, and all he said when he was done was "Godfrey, what a wind!"

Lucy and I agreed. It was a cold wind, and it raved in our faces as we plodded, with coats held tight and milk pails rattling, between the Owl Pen and the goat

pen, a-choring bound. The sun was setting. The western
sky was filled with blood and fire, and huge black skudding
clouds. The northern sky was as coldly green as a sunlit
polar sea. The pine trees soughed and twisted. The elm
trees shuddered their branches like skeletons in a dance.

Somehow that evening as we rounded up our wind-
ruffled chickens and put them safely to bed, as we drove
our protesting ducks into their snug quarters, as we herded
our screaming geese into their big pen, our choring seemed
less humble, less mundane than usual. We felt ourselves
part of an age-old battle. Somehow we felt that we ourselves were warring with the elements, fighting a primeval
fight. We were cave folk. We screamed, mimicking our
geese. We shouted our defiance to the gods that rode the
storm.

Up the long hillside we went, up to the windswept hill
top and the old stone wall that is there. We stood with
our feet wide apart and our backs bent, breasting the gale,
looking down over darkening miles of storm-swept countryside, down on a strangley different Owl Pen and a changed
Moonstone Creek. We looked and stared. The old familiar
scene below was strangely new, and newly strange.

A weird half-light filled the valley with a ruddy glow.
Trees and barns and farm houses gleamed as though touched
by fire. They cast fantastic shadows, long twisty scrawly
things, such as goblins or witches might cast. Our chicken
house looked lost, small, and lonely. The fields below
were not our fields, not the fields we knew. It might well
have been a lost valley in the moon that we gazed on,
and yet it was home. Clouds covered the sunset, and a
sudden squall of rain hid even the fences in the next field.
Our faces dripped.

It was still raining when Lucy and I went to bed that
night. We lay in the darkness, listening to the wind-driven
drops beat on the slanting ceiling of our room, on the

shingles overhead. They pattered like little animal feet. They pecked like birds. They sang. They danced. They ran. Sometimes they were like little fingers beating out a tune. We lay in the darkness, listening, thinking . . .

Tomorrow, we knew, would be just another day. In the morning when the first light of dawn crooked like a rosy finger in the eastern sky, we would get out of bed and open our doors on a quiet, rainwashed world. We would pick up our feed buckets, and climb the hillside, a-choring bound again. Again, we would say "hello" to Beefy, our pet rooster, and to Dirty Back, our pet hen. Again, we would hear the distant voice of a farm girl calling cattle home . . . the bark of a dog . . . the quack of a duck . . . the whispered laughter of Moonstone Creek.

# PART 13

## Where Drinks the Beast

Happy the man, whose wish and care
A few paternal acres bound,
Content to breath his native air
In his own ground.

Whose herds with milk, whose fields with bread,
Whose flocks supply him with attire;
Whose trees in summer yield him shade,
In winter fire . . .

ALEXANDER POPE, 1688

# 37

## We Champion Goats

THERE IS ON MOONSTONE CREEK, JUST BELOW THE LITTLE bridge that carries the tenth concession over it, a pretty little pool. In the springtime a man can usually find a trout in it. In the summertime, unless he is careful to announce his coming by loud whistling, he is just as likely to find his neighbour's wife or daughter crouched there, trying to cover her large nakedness with a small cake of soap or a wash cloth. In a dry fall it is a favourite watering place for cattle, and the gray plank bridge railings, put up to keep the beasts from breaking down the embankment, make a good place to sit while they drink.

Somehow, it is not possible for two men to stand, or sit, together on a bridge and watch cattle drink, without getting into a discussion of some kind. Last fall was no exception. Enough words of wisdom fell from Moonstone Bridge to rile the water. The talk ranged from how atomic energy might be used to spread manure, to talk about goats in general and our two goats, Suzanne and Josephine, in particular.

Goats are unpleasant, our neighbours insisted. They are ugly. They are destructive. They smelled. They are useless. They didn't like goats. Lucy and I battled grimly. We carried the standard of goatdom into wordy war. We answered attack with counter-attack, and thrust with parry. We led with an upper cut to their cows, and followed with a right hook to their bulls. We thought of getting a lawyer.

Compared to a goat, we argued, a cow is a filthy thing, a great big lumbering manure wagon that no self-respecting goat will graze after in a pasture field. A cow will lie down in its own droppings. A goat will not. A cow will eat its own bedding. A goat will starve first. A cow will allow itself to become fouled with its own manure. A goat is always spotlessly clean. Compared to a goat, the best of cows is unutterably stupid. A goat can be taught any trick that a dog can be taught, and will develop an affection for its owner unequalled by any other beast. A cow, we thundered, cannot even be taught to come in out of the rain.

Yet it is always the cow that is shown as the benefactor of mankind, we complained. The story book widow always has a cow, never a goat. This, in the face of the fact that for tens of thousands of years before mankind degenerated into dependence on the larger, untidier beast, it was the goat, and the goat alone, that provided man with his milk, and meat, butter, and cheese. This, in the face of the fact that the best cheeses are still made of goat's milk, that goat's milk is completely free of those dangerous disease organisims which force pasteurization of a cow's milk upon our cities, that the goats themselves are untouched by the majority of the diseases which infest cattle.

"The best glove leather is still made from goat skins," said Lucy.

"And young roast goat is to roast veal what fine wine is to bilge water," said I.

We told our listeners that a nanny goat has less smell to her than a cow, and that what smell there is, is sweeter. We did not bother to add that the most pestiferously reeking beast in creation is a billy goat in the breeding season. Frankness never yet won an argument. We hurried on to the more important point that five nanny goats can be kept in the space required by one cow, and maintained on one cow's ration.

"A really good milch goat will give up to six quarts of milk a day," I summed up, not once but a dozen times! "Multiply that by five and you have thirty quarts of milk flowing into your bucket every twenty-four hours. How many cows in Medonte will beat that?"

"How many quarts a day do your two beasts give?" asked Farmer Jim one sunny day.

"What's that got to do with it?" I wanted to know.

"Just tell me," insisted Jim.

"Well, about half a pint, if you must know," I confessed.

"Each?" Jim smiled.

"All told," I scowled.

"That's why you carry a pail up the road to my cow byre each night?"

"Yes."

"Well," said Farmer Jim, "that's why I keep cows."

But such argument, we insisted, was not fair. Our goats, lovely ladies though they were, were not good milch goats. They were neither registered, accredited, pure-bred, or R.O.P. They were simply goats, nice goats, that came to us as gifts from an owner who had tired of their fence-jumping proclivities, and who, when she found herself unable to break them of the habit, determined to get rid of them before they taught the rest of the herd their bad tricks.

We liked our goats, and we were grateful for the gift of them, (that for the record) but we did not want all goatdom judged by them. Nor did we want this stressing of their defects to blind a beholder to their many virtues. They were deer-like, and amiable. When let out of their stall they would leap lightly into the milking stand, and stand there like rocks until we had finished milking them. It was not fair, we held, to detract from their willingness to co-operate by pointing out that they did not have to stand for long. They stood as long as was required. Like the widow who gave her mite, they gave what they had freely, even eagerly. They gave their all.

About this point in the argument, Lucy and I would invariably find ourselves half-way home, walking across the side hill pasture to the goat pen, talking to ourselves. Someday, we have decided, someday when Jo and Sue are mere memories that linger with us in the shape of an useless electric fence, and a pair of fine goatskin rugs, we will have goats at Owl Pen that will silence forever those ribald joke masters who sit like crows in the autumn of the year on the rails by Moonstone Creek. Someday we'll take a pair of milk-proud nannies slumming, right into their dark cow byres. We'll match their ruddy moo-cows, squirt for squirt, and bah for moo. We'll show them! Maybe . . .

# 38

## *We Buy More Bees*

NOVEMBER WAS BEING KITTENISH, EVEN SILLY. THERE were violets blooming by Moonstone Creek. Great fat fronds of pussy-willows were waving in the big swamp back of Bass Lake. Dandelions bloomed on the Owl Pen lawn, and the Owl Pen well was dry of an almost summer-like drought. Farmer Jim, with his shirt open at the neck and his hat shoved well back on his head, drove his cattle every day down the dusty concession line to water at the pool by the bridge.

"When I get these brutes back home, I'm taking my brother-in-law's truck and going after some cattle beasts that are on pasture back of Coldwater," he told me one morning as I stood beside him on the bridge, watching his herd slip and scramble down the steep bank to the water's edge. "Fellow who owns them wants them home before the weather changes, and I guess this crazy weather can't last many days more."

We watched the beasts, knee deep in creek water, drinking their fill. We watched a glinting procession of honey bees fly down to drink with them. We heard a bluejay, and a chickadee, and saw a butterfly. It was the sort of day to make a man dream of a long road and a far hill, the sort of day to make even a king envy a man the chance of gadding down a concession line in a red truck, with a load of bawling cattle and a panting collie dog.

"You'd better come with me," said Jim.

I did try to say no. There was so much work to be done, work in the chicken house, in the goat pen, in the wood yard, and in the honey house; but Jim pointed out that he would be travelling right past a bee-yard where there were bees for sale. I had talked by telephone with the owner of those bees. They were supposed to be good bees, in new hives, on new comb, and with new bottom and cover boards. We did need more bees if we were to stock our new yard by Coulson Mill pond in the spring. It would be a simple matter to throw twenty or twenty-five hives on the back of the truck after the cattle were unloaded.

"I shouldn't," I murmured, weakly.

Noon found us miles from Owl Pen, rolling down a sandy side road through a range of wooded hills. We were rid of our cattle. The truck floor behind us was spread with a thick layer of fresh straw, ready for the bees we were to buy. We turned at a cross-road by a red brick church, and slid with squealing brakes down a break-neck bit of hill. Soon we would be at the bee-yard. I ransacked my brain trying to remember all the things that I had read a man should do and watch for when buying bees.

Part of my job in picking out the colonies we were to bring home with us would be to make sure that the majority of those million bees were young. It was important that even the queen in each hive should be no more than a year old. Every last bee had to be free of disease. The comb had to be sound worker comb and free from drone cells, and packed with light honey or sugar syrup sufficient to feed the bees through the long winter ahead, and through early spring until blossoming fruit trees and flowers gave the bees a chance to gather new food for themselves.

"This is a lucky break for Lucy and me," I told Jim, as we rolled along. "Getting these hives all new and freshly painted means that we will be able to do a bit of skiing this winter, see a bit of the countryside, instead of squatting in a workshop with a hammer and a paint brush."

The coloured miles slipped by. We picked up the bee-man at his home, a pretty house on a side hill with a savage dog chained beside the door. I was properly diffident. This was no mere beginner in bee-keeping like myself. This was an old-timer, an expert, a professional. This was a man who played with hundreds of hives, and no mere fifty, such as we had at Owl Pen.

"How many colonies have you?" he asked, as he crowded into the cab beside us.

"Fifty," I told him, rather apologetically.

He smiled.

I told him of the work that Lucy and I had put in on our fifty hives, how we had painted and repainted them, and tarred their bottoms to keep out damp, and fitted each front with a distinctively coloured alighting board so that our bees would have no difficulty in finding their way to their own hives. He smiled again. I told him how we had numbered our hives, choosing Roman numerals, and a good shade of red paint. He chuckled. I shut up. After all, he was the professional, the expert, the bee-master. I was the beginner. I resolved to miss nothing in his bee-yard, to learn what I could.

Following the bee-man's directions, Jim wheeled the truck off the highway which we were now travelling, and down a concession line. We turned on to a side road, and then down another concession line. We stopped, and let down some cattle bars, and then bumped along a rutty lane. Some sickly-looking cows mooed at us. Some runty poplars scraped the side of the truck. We stopped again. We had arrived.

I got out of the truck and stood by a barbed wire fence. I said nothing. I had nothing to say. The hives I had travelled so far to see stood laid out in three or four long rows in front of me. Except for their orderly arrangement a passer-by might have mistaken them for a collection of long-abandoned soap boxes. Some of them had

been painted years before. Others had never been painted
at all. All were weathered gray, checked and cracked.
None were on hive stands, scraps of rotten inch lumber
being all that stood between them and the damp ground.
The covers, many of which were red with rust, had been
jammed down over old feed bags, the tattered overlapping
edges of which flapped sadly in the wind.

I walked into the centre of the yard and stopped hap-
hazardly at a hive. It looked no better, and no worse,
than any of the others. Standing straddle-legged over it,
I slipped my hands into the grip holes and hefted it. It
was heavy, weighing close to seventy pounds. That was
something. I slipped off the weathered cover. It was dripping wet on the inside. I peeled back the sodden feed bag,
exposing ten rows of brown-black comb. They were crowded,
and the box was literally crammed, with finely coloured
bees.

"They are all the same," put in the bee-keeper. "They
are all strong colonies. They have all been fed. They'll
all winter well and come out strong in the spring."

"Are they all healthy?" I wanted to know.

I was assured that they were, that they had all been
inspected and found free of disease.

I don't suppose that if the day had not been what it
was, if we had not travelled so far, and if the season had
not been so advanced as to make this my last chance to
buy established colonies that fall, I would have bought at
at all. Certainly the equipment was not what I had expected it to be, and yet there was, after all, nothing
wrong with it that nails, paint and putty would not make
right. Another winter in the workshop loomed ahead.

"Sold," I decided, in a voice that was entirely lacking
in the enthusiasm I had expected to feel on such an
occasion.

Jim backed the red truck up to the edge of the yard.
The bee-man prepared little scraps of wire screening with

which to close the entrances of the hives I chose to buy. I made my way up and down the long rows, picking out of the seventy-five odd hives in the yard the twenty-five that I wanted.

If a hive appeared sound and in reasonably good condition, I lifted it off the ground. If it was heavy enough to suggest that it was loaded with bees and honey, I opened it. If every frame was covered with bees, if the frames were loaded with capped honey, if the bees seemed contented and at peace with themselves and the world, I closed it again, laid a twig on the cover board, and passed on. Soon there were twenty-five hives scattered about the bee-yard, with bits of wood on their covers, and with bits of wire screening closing their entrances. They roared as we picked them up. They roared as we loaded them on the truck. They roared again, a million loud bee voices strong, as we turned the truck towards home.

It was dark when we arrived at the Owl Pen, dark except for the pale glimmer of an old moon, and the glint of frost on the gate. We carried the still roaring hives from the truck to the work yard, and laid them out in three long rows by the wood pile.

"Where are you going to put them for the winter?" asked Lucy, who had come down to watch the unloading, lantern in hand.

"In the cellar," I answered.

"My cellar!" Lucy's voice arose in an ascending tremolo, "among my fruit and vegetables where I have to go every day? Do you mean to say that even in the winter-time I won't be able to get away from your howling, buzzing bees?"

"There's just a million of them," I comforted.

"A million bees!" The light of Lucy's lantern grew small and faint as she made her way back up the hill to the house. "A million bees in my cellar! A million bees between me and my jam!"

# 39

## *We Go to the Fair*

"HEIGH-HO, COME TO THE FAIR!"

So go the words of the old song. So went the words down the rain-swept concession lines of Medonte. They crowded the more usual gossip off the party telephone lines. They ran like a whisper of wind in the willows along the banks of the Coldwater River. They swept up Moonstone Valley. They mingled with the waters of Moonstone Creek, until every little waterfall and rapids seemed to be singing, over and over again, "Heigh-heigh-ho-ho-come-to-the-fair!"

At least that is the way that Lucy and I like to think that the idea of visiting the fair came to us. We had made no plans for such a journey. We had saved no egg money to such an end. We were keeping Beefy, our pet rooster, decently at home. The idea came to us out of the blue, so to speak, or perhaps out of the singing creek water that we were drinking because our well was dry. We invited our friends and neighbours to a Sunday tea.

Inviting neighbours in to tea is, unless one has a hired man, an essential country prelude to an overnight journey. Someone must be found to look after the stock, to feed and milk the goats, to feed the chickens and gather the eggs, to water the ducks, and throw hay to the geese. Lucy brought out her best silver teapot and made sandwiches of an extra special kind. I put away the tobacco and papers that we ordinarily use, and put in a supply of ready-made cigarettes, and a handful of the best eleven cent cigars to be had at the corner store.

Casually, ever so casually, as we handed around our best tea cups, we mentioned the fair. We would like to go to the fair we said, but there were goats, and ducks, and chickens, and geese, and . . . well . . . Our neighbours clucked sympathetically, reached for some more sandwiches, and said nothing. Livestock are such a tie, we sighed.

"Worse than babies," agreed a friend, at last. "You can take a baby into a hotel with you, but even boarding houses object to a goat."

"And we have two," I moaned. "Have a cigar?"

"Imagine what they would say at the Royal York if we turned up with our ducks!" put in Lucy.

"Imagine what the ducks would say!" grinned a neighbour, and took a cigar.

Our neighbours are the longest-suffering folk in Medonte. Two of them left that evening with our two goats, Suzanne and Josephine, bleating in the back of their family sedan. Two others left with the keys to our chicken house. A third left with a hamper that meowed. Our dog Thunder we planned to take with us. Heigh-ho, the deed was done. All was set for the fair.

We had several reasons for wanting to go to the Royal Winter Fair. For one thing, we wanted to see if the Chanticler chickens on display were any better than our Chanticlers. We wanted to see if the cockerels on show were any better than our pal, Beefy. We wanted to see the Rouen and mallard ducks, and the Toulouse and Canada geese. We wanted to see Canada's best in these breeds so that we might have, in the future, a standard by which to judge our own.

We might as well have stayed at home. To say this is not even to suggest that there were not fine birds at the fair. Simple justice compels us to admit that the geese we saw there were bigger, and heavier, and more impressively dewlapped and keeled than any that strut on the hillside above the Owl Pen. The Rouen ducks were brighter of plumage, and meatier by far than any of ours. But for plain friendliness and good nature, for nice character and lovable disposition, ours were beyond compare with anything we saw on show. We insisted upon that. It may be, of course, that we were a bit prejudiced. It may be that we were not inclined to admit, even to ourselves, imperfection in our friends.

We felt better when we came to the cages that house the Chanticler exhibit. At first we were almost afraid to look. Then we peeked. Phooey! Our friend Beefy topped the lot. The cockerels in the cages were mere shadows of what Beefy might have been had he been stepped on as an egg. And the pullets! Phooey again! Dirty Back, our pet pullet, would have cried for a bathing suit and a chance to strut had she seen the miserable competition that was hers at the Royal Winter Fair. We were glad that she didn't. The sight might have given her ideas, ideas that have nothing at all to do with the simple life, and a simple little nest—at home.

They say that there is intoxication in success. Certainly Lucy and I were more than slightly elated as we walked from the poultry show into the farm implement section. Our chickens went to our heads. Thinking of Beefy, we felt expansive. Thinking of Dirty Back, we determined to expand. Nothing was too good for our Chanticlers. We stopped by a poultry appliance exhibit and priced the latest thing in oil burning brooder stoves, in electrically heated water fountains, in food hoppers and ventilator cowls. At home we would have shuddered at the price of the cheapest of them. At the fair, we ordered the lot.

"Do you want to pay now?" asked the salesman.

I clutched the dollar and a half in my pocket. "Send

collect," I whispered. "Send collect," I repeated a little weakly.

We went to another booth, where a garden tractor, resplendent in yellow, blue, and bright red paint, stood gloriously among potted palms. Once again we thought of our magnificent Beefy, our lovely Dirty Back. That tractor was just the thing for turning over the soil in chicken runs that needed freshening, for ploughing and reseeding a poultry range. We really needed a tractor, we told ourselves, and enquired as to prices and available equipment. We did mental arithmetic, and a little rapid calculation on the back of a cigarette box. Easy! At our present rate of production our eggs would pay for such a machine (equipped, of course), in a mere thirty-three years.

The salesman took our name and address.

Still the fatal intoxication engendered by that long look we had taken at the inferior cockerel in the poultry show drove us on. Our next stop was at the automobile exhibit. A splendid station wagon stood on an oriental carpet. A radio played sweet music. Pretty girls, hired, I suspect, for the occasion, lolled on near-by settees. An admiring crowd stood around. A salesman, who looked like a movie star, and who spoke like a radio announcer, extolled its merits. It may be that somebody pushed us. The next moment we, who had managed for over a year with a red wheel barrow as our only means of transportation, were sitting in that car.

"Quite reasonable," I heard myself saying to the salesman.

"Just what we want," said Lucy, a dewy, dreamy, drippy look writ large on her shining face.

Somehow the green-faced gods of country living who watch over us in Medonte, managed to reach out of their native hills just in time to prevent me from taking my fountain pen out of my pocket. It may be that they knew that my cheque book was in the same pocket. They may also have known that my account book showed a credit balance of less than two dollars. They may have known, being gods, that the writing of a cheque for over two thousand dollars is, under such circumstances, sheer fraud, punishable by imprisonment.

"I think we had better get out of here," said Lucy.

We left, by way of the tractor exhibit, where we cancelled our order for one tractor, (equipped), and by way of the poultry appliance display, where we cancelled all but one item on our order there. We had almost spent $3,180.10. We had actually spent $10.18. For some folk a log house on a concession line, ten miles from the nearest town, and eighty-five miles from a fair, is the safest place to be.

# PART 14

## Snow Drifts For Two

"... I sat down in my bath upon a sheet of thick ice which broke in the middle ... not particularly comforting to naked thighs and loins for the keen ice cut like fire ... I had to collect the pieces and pile them on a chair before I could use the sponge ..."

FRANCIS KILVERT, 1870

# 40

## *We Welcome Winter*

WINTER CAME TO MEDONTE RIDING PICK-A-BACK ON A WIND
that howled like a tom cat in the leafless branches of the
elm trees. There was no snow at first, just the wind—
cold and wet and comfortless. Every living thing scurried
for cover. Birds disappeared from the cedar trees. Even
the jack-rabbits left their upland pastures, and came skulk-
ing down to the bottom lands at dusk to spend the night
in the shelter of the steep banks of Moonstone Creek.

It was the sort of night that called for hot cocoa, and
a big fire. Lucy and I piled log on log until the black
chimney of the Owl Pen fireplace roared its own wild
answer to the wilder wind without. We put extra wood
in the kitchen stove, and a small fire in the upstairs stove,
and a folded rag rug over the crack at the bottom of the

north door. We drank our cocoa and blinked our eyes. On such a night thoughts of bed come early to country folk. It was half-past eight when we turned out the lights.

If we had any doubts, as we snuggled into bed that night, as to what change the wind was bringing to our world, we had none when we awoke next morning. We knew, even before we opened our eyes, that winter, long overdue, had come at last. Our noses were cold. The room was cold. Our three cats were piled in a purring, heat-loving tangle on top of us. Thunder, our pup, was curled into a small shivering ball on the rug beside the bed.

"The fires have burned out," said Lucy. "I'm glad I'm not a man."

It was just breaking day. I went to the window and rubbed a hole in the strange, white frost flowers that covered every pane. The wind had died. The world was utterly still, and white, and beautiful. The thin red light of dawn showed familiar trees and shrubs touched to new loveliness by snow that clung to every limb, and branch, and twig, changing the plain wood of them to silver filigree. Pines and cedars, weighed down by great masses of the clinging whiteness, seemed suddenly no trees at all but white-robed giants and friars out of old books, lost and changed to statues on our hills.

Nothing, it seemed to me as I stood there shivering at the frost-clouded window, was too mean or humble for winter's transmuting touch. The wire fences about our chicken house were changed to screens of fairy lace. The electric cables running from the Owl Pen to the goat house were grown into fat silver festoons that sagged in lovely, sweeping curves across our pasture field. They shivered ever so slightly as the dawn breeze touched them, and I shivered too. There were ducks, and geese, and chickens, and goats at the far end of those lovely festoons. All were hungry. All were waiting to be fed.

I pulled on socks that felt like fly screens, and boots that felt like tin, and went down stairs. Thunder, who knew his every morning fate, followed reluctantly. I opened the front door and thrust him out into the dawn-lit whiteness. The three cats followed, after I had dragged them by the scruff of their protesting necks from under chairs, and tables, and bookcases. Why dogs and cats, after centuries of domestication, and human companionship, should remain utterly unable to cope with indoor plumbing, is one of the mysteries of life that I often ponder.

There remained, before I went out to the chicken house, the lighting of the fires. On a warm morning, when there is really no need of a fire at all, fire lighting is child's play. Then even the dampest stick of green poplar will flare, on the slightest provocation, like a sliver of fat pine. Kindling is not needed. One match does the trick. But let frost whiten the door latch, and there is a different tale to tell.

On a cold morning, when the room is cold, and the stove is cold, and frost crystals crawl like white mice in one's underwear, then the devil himself would be stumped to get a lively fire blazing at Owl Pen. It is a matter then of care, and prayer, and solemn, purposeful cursing. It is a matter then of whittling fine wood finer, of using matches by the score, of huffing and puffing. Everything smokes, and nothing burns. It is a matter of shouting answers to shouted questions up a smoke-filled stairway.

"No, Lucy, the house is not on fire. Please go back to sleep."

"No, Lucy, I'm not swearing at you; I'm swearing at myself. Please go back to sleep!"

"No, Lucy, I haven't gone crazy. It is just that these (incoherent chewing sound) fires won't start. Please go back to sleep!"

"No, Lucy, I didn't kick the dog. The dog is outside.

If you must know, I YELLED BECAUSE I CUT MY-SELF! PLEASE GO BACK TO SLEEP!"

It was nice to get out of the smoke-filled house, out into the shoutless, unresentful quiet of the dawn. As I waded through the new snow, with a steaming pailful of warm water bumping against my right leg, and sploshing into my right rubber boot, I noticed that the snow shadows cast by the slowly rising sun had fine blue and rose-pink edges. My neighbour's house, seen across the snow-covered fields through a delicate tracery of snow-covered alder branches, was a farm house no longer. It was, in the coloured light of a winter's dawning, like an elfin hunting lodge. A plume of woodsmoke rose lazily from the furthest chimney.

All around me, wherever I looked, other blue-gray pennons of quiet smoke were drifting skyward. Some rose from the chimneys of farm houses not over a quarter of a mile distant. Others rose from houses hidden by wood or hills. They seemed like giant feathers in the sky. Other fire-lighters had cursed as I had. Other wives had questioned. I was not alone, either in my troubles or in my earliness. Other pails of water were being carried up other hillsides, to other barns and chicken houses. Other solitary men were standing like myself on other lonely footpaths, wondering at the beauty of the day. Other rubber boots were, quite possibly, as sodden as my own.

But beauty and wet feet are not the only reward a farmer gets for early rising on a winter's day. A countryman gets more out of the dawn than a few minutes of day dreaming on a barnyard path with a bucket in his hand. His real reward comes when the bucket is delivered, when he opens his barn, or chicken house door on a host of dependant living things that ba-a-h, and moo, and whinney, and cluck their recognition, their welcome, and delight.

My reward came that way, with the clangour of small

hooves on the goat pen floor as I set my bucket down in the snow, preparatory to opening the door. It came with Jo's soft ba-a-h as I opened the door, and with Sue's bright-eyed demand for hay, more hay, and oats, lots of oats. It came with the defiant hiss of our grey geese, and the questioning quornk of our Canada geese, with the hysterical gabble of our ducks, and the comfortable cluck-a-cluck of our hens.

So to the feeding—hay and oats, as demanded, for the goats, grain in water for the geese, and the same for the ducks, grain, and mash, and oyster shell for the hens. The mash bin is nearly empty. Make a note of that. We will need more grain soon. Make a note of that. Lug out manure. Lug in fresh straw for litter and bedding. Tidy up each pen and stall. Set a lighted lantern under the wall pump to keep out the frost. Milk Jo, and feed her milk to Sue, who is a bit off colour. Pet Beefy, the pet rooster, and Dirty Back, the pet hen. And then, for five minutes at least, stand in the breast-warmed dimness doing nothing at all.

What if breakfast is waiting down the hillside in the old timber house by the creek? Breakfast will wait, and so will Lucy. So will Alice at Plum Tree Farm, while Farmer Jim stands awhile in his warm barn, listening to the rhythmic munch-munch-munch of his cattle eating hay, to the rustle of the fresh straw that they tread. Breakfast will wait too at North Rising Farm, while the man of the house there leans quietly on his pig pen rail, listening to the happy suck-suck-and-squeal of baby porkers, and the comfortable grunting of their dam. It waits on every farm every winter morning of the year.

Breakfast waited an especially long time at Owl Pen the morning winter came. Lucy came to the Owl Pen door and shouted. I did not hear her. I had ears only for the small, happy feeding sounds of our small birds and beasts. The warmth of summer was in the beast-warmed air. The sweetness of summer was in their breath, and in the straw, and clover hay piled nearby. There was a rustling everywhere that spoke of summer fields. I was making a discovery, a great discovery. I was privy at last to every farmer's secret. Though cold wind blow, though snowdrifts grow, summer is never further from a farm house than the stable door.

# 41

*We Walk for Milk*

PLUM TREE FARM IS UPHILL FROM OWL PEN. IT LOOKS down through a screen of elm trees at our little log house by Moonstone Creek, and we look up at it over old rail fences and tumbled stone walls. The road between is a familiar road to Lucy and me, for every day, through all the changing seasons of a year, we walked it with milk pails swinging in our hands.

I don't suppose that if the old sow at North Rising Farm had not had a litter of nine little pigs when she did that we would ever have started thinking of ways and means of avoiding this jaunt. They were nice little pigs, intelligent people.

"You notice that they keep their milk supply handy," said their owner one day as we bent over the top bar of their pen, watching them take a between-meal snack from their obliging dam.

We did. It started us thinking. We decided that what pigs could do we, with a bit of trying, might manage too. We built ourselves a goat house, and fitted it with box stalls, standing stalls, and a milking stand. We got two goats, Suzanne and Josephine, and told Farmer Jim of Plum Tree that he and his wife, Alice, would be seeing a lot less of us.

It was not that the milk was not good, or that the price was not right, we explained. It was not that we minded the walk from Owl Pen to Plum Tree in the springtime of the year when the way was sweet with violets and blossoming pin cherry trees. Even a glimpse through pelting rain of a spray of hawthorne blossoms against an old rail fence was more than enough to make up for a wet back and muddy shoes. The gray dust of summer was a mere nothing when it was filled with the music of lowing cattle, and the fragrance of new mown hay. We pointed out that we did not mind the walk in the autumn of the year either. There was the red of the maple, and the gold of the birch, and the fat nuts of the beech trees to reward the walker on the concession line then. It was the winter walk we wanted to avoid, we explained, and Farmer Jim understood.

It seems now that it was our goats that we should have taken into our confidence—not the farmer. It was our goats that let us down. During all the glorious days of summer, when even a town store keeper might have enjoyed a walk on our concession line, our nannies gave us milk in abundance. They gave us enough for ourselves, and for Thunder, and for Titch, and Skudger, and Bumps. Like the little pigs in the pen at the cross roads farm, we had our milk supply handy. Like them we stayed at home. In the autumn the beech nuts and the wild grapes on the hillside knew us not, and neither did the autumn rains.

"Ah," we told ourselves, "we are clever, as clever as little pigs."

We were not particularly perturbed when, as the days passed, our milk supply began decreasing a little. We read no warning in our goats' increasing restlessness. Goats will be goats, we mused, and milked them as usual, night and morning, and fed them as usual, three times a day. How were we to know, or even guess that our nannies were telling us, as clearly as they could, that though we milked them and fed them we were neglecting them, that their hearts were broken, that they were lonely, that they wanted love?

So winter came, and so Suzanne went dry. Storms filled

our concession line waist deep, fence deep, and sometimes chin deep. Josephine went dry. Once again our lantern blinked in the wind on the hillside. Once again our milk pails tinkled in the dark of winter evenings. Once again we climbed, every other night, through the tall snow drifts that lie between Owl Pen and Plum Tree. It seemed to us that we never needed milk before a storm, or after a storm. We always needed it the night of a storm. As sure as a snow-filled wind yelled out of the northwest, our pitchers would be empty.

And yet, somehow, it was fun. It was nice stumbling off the drifted concession line into Farmer Jim's kitchen. I don't think there is anything on earth to compare with the warm good cheer and comfort of a farm house kitchen on a stormy winter night. To rumble out of howling, frost-filled darkness into a cosy lamp-lit room that smells of burning wood and homemade bread is to know the meaning of that old phrase which has to do with heaven being on earth. If farm house smells aren't in heaven, paradise will be a dead loss to me.

The lamplight gleaming from the kitchen window at Plum Tree was always our beacon, our lode star, as we climbed the long hillside. We aimed for it, come hell or high drifts, and stamped down the rutted lane past it to the woodshed door.

"Brush me off," was Lucy's invariable, breathless order when we got there.

I would put down my lantern, and take up the corn broom that always stood by the door and sweep her, as one would a rug, from head to foot. Then she would take the broom and sweep me. We even made a habit of sweeping our dog Thunder, for he is a big dog and can carry a lot of snow, and Alice does not like snow water on her kitchen floor. Long before we were finished, Jim would be at the door with the lamp.

"Come on in," he would boom.

We never needed a second invitation. In we would go to find Alice seated by the stove with a lap full of socks. She would smile quietly as we came in, and go on with her darning. We knew why she smiled. We knew why Farmer Jim was smiling as he closed the door behind us. We had said too much about our goats. We had bragged too loudly about our independance of Plum Tree and its cows. We had argued too wildly by Moonstone Creek.

"How are your goats?" asked Jim, night after night, as we loosened our coats, and put two more chairs by the stove.

"Have a cigarette," was my stock reply.

"Go on, tell us how the funny little things are," Alice would invariably urge.

Always when Lucy and I stamped with our dog and our pails into the kitchen at Plum Tree we told ourselves that we were only going to stay five minutes. Maybe ten minutes. No more. Always we stayed an hour, and some-times more than an hour, eating apples, gossiping, frying our feet against the stove fender, dreading the walk back home. We always knew when the party was over.

"Gol," Jim would say, heaving himself out of his chair, and putting another stick on the fire. "If it gets much worse out, you'll have to stay the night."

That was the signal. Up we would get, and button our coats. Lucy usually wrapped her scarf around her head and ears so that only her eyes showed through. My burden was the milk; her's was the lantern. Usually Jim saw us to the door again.

"A lovely night!" was his usual parting comment, that and a grin as our lantern guttered and flickered in the wind, threatening to go out. "I'll bet you two will be sorry when spring comes round again!"

Never again will Lucy and I stand between goats and romance.

# 42

## *We Shiver in Bed*

LUCY AND I HUDDLED AND CLUNG TOGETHER IN BED, TOO cold to sleep. We wondered where the draft was coming from. The solid pine timbers of our old house seemed changed to cheese cloth. The wind soughed and sucked through every room. It slithered up our twisty wooden stairs into our bedroom and into our bed, into my pyjamas and Lucy's nightdress. Our feet congealed. Our noses shrank. Our ears grew numb.

"It must be terrible outside," chattered Lucy.

"Bad," I quavered in reply.

It wouldn't have been so bad if we had gone to bed in a warm house. But we hadn't. It would have been better if I had put a decent fire into the fireplace and stoves before going to bed. But I didn't. It would have been still better if the big front door of our house hadn't blown open after we went to bed, and stayed open the rest of the night. But it did.

Winter had its way with our happy home that night. In the morning there was six inches of snow on the living room floor. Some dregs in a teacup on the table were frozen into a lump of evil-looking ice. An apple on the mantel shelf was changed to iron. Our three cats had deserted the place entirely, and gone crawling through the tempest a quarter of a mile to the comparative warmth and shelter of a distant barn. Only Thunder, our pup, had stayed with us, whining with discomfort. He, poor devil, didn't know where the barn was.

It did not take me long to dress. My fingers literally

blurred over my buttons. My socks went on with a rocket-like br-r-r-p. I remembered as I pulled on my trousers, that I had not taken off my pyjamas. It didn't matter. I pulled on a sweater, and then, as an after-thought, put a tweed jacket on over it.

My fires did well by me that morning. They were one-match fires, every one of them. It was no time at all before I was standing with my back to a flame-filled fireplace, feeling the beautiful heat eat into my spine, and smelling the soul-satisfying reek of burning wool, as my backside grew red hot. I stood and pondered the night, and the storm in the night.

It had not been a particularly bad storm, not really. The drifts, as I could see from the living room window, were not more than four, or six feet high. The temperature had dropped to a mere three, or four below zero. It was the wind, I supposed, that had made things seem so grim —the wind and a pound of bacon.

Yesterday had been fair. The snow-plough had come down our concession line, and with it word that some particularly nice bacon was to be had at a certain store in town. We needed groceries. We appreciate good bacon. And bacon and a ploughed road are not an everyday occurrance in Medonte in the winter time.

As we reached town, it began to snow. We knew the signs. We rushed through our shopping, and were half-way home again when it began to blow. It grew dark. We crawled along through a fog of swirling whiteness that our headlights could not pierce. The drifts grew, and reached long smooth tongues out from the roadside fence rows. The ruts filled. The road disappeared.

Still all might have been well if the car we were riding in had not then decided to develop a clogged feed line. It coughed and sputtered. It wheezed and died. The owner assured us that it had never done that before. We believed him. A snow drift grew over the front bumper, and over the headlights. The battery gave out. The heater refused to work. We sat glumly, staring ahead into a white nothingness, with frost eating into our bones, and the bacon in my overcoat pocket.

"Sooner or later another car, or something, will come along," comforted the driver. "In the meantime, let's have music."

He turned on the radio.

"Let it snow. Let it snow. Let it snow." blatted some silly crooner in a distant, steam-heated radio station.

We spun the dial.

"Oh, the weather outside is frightful . . . "

We spun it again.

"In a winter wonderland . . . "

We turned the crazy gadget off.

The drifts continued to grow. It was quite obvious that within another half-hour at most the road would be blocked completely. We thought of telephoning a neighbour to come for us with his horses, as we were only two and a half miles from home, but it seemed a shame to call a man or beast out into the bitter darkness of such a night. But what to do? A glow grew in the blackness behind us. A truck came pitching and slewing through the deep snow. It was going our way.

Lucy and I arrived home, chilled to the marrow, and as hungry as bears. The house was cold, for all the fires had been out for hours. It was untidy, for our dog and three cats had been locked in too long. We let them out, and tidied up the mess they had made. We thought uneasily of our unfed goats, and hens, and ducks, and geese. There was nothing we could do for them before morning. They would not eat in the dark. We fed our pets, ate a sandwich, and shivered into bed.

Getting off to a bad start with a winter storm doesn't

pay, I told myself, as I took the incandescent seat of my trousers away from the roaring fireplace, and out across the pasture field to the goat pen. A bad start, they say, makes a bad finish. I wasn't at all surprised to find the pump in the goat house frozen, and the water buckets filled with ice.

"This finishes it," I gritted, as I battered the ice out of them with a heavy hammer. "Nothing more can happen. Everything has happened. Absolutely everything."

I had one thought to comfort me. It would be warm in the Owl Pen by the time I got back to it. The huge logs I had piled into the fireplace would be burning merrily. The stove in the kitchen would be gleaming cherry red. The whole place would be filled with the fine, sweet smell of coffee and frying bacon. I hurried through the last of my chores and gathered up the eggs, then pulled my parka closer about my ears and turned towards home.

A long black pennon of smoke was crawling lazily along the pine tree tops. My eyes chased along it, back to the Owl Pen chimney. Tongues of flame were spouting skyward. The chimney was like a volcano, spouting fire, smoke, and ashes in great flaming gouts. Only the lava was missing. Glowing cinders were falling in a thick red rain on the roof. There were ashes everywhere. I had warmed the place up all right. I had set it on fire!

Somewhere between the chicken house and the Owl Pen I dropped the eggs. I don't know where. My mind wasn't on eggs. I raced to the Owl Pen and flung open the door. The house was filled with a sullen roaring sound. There was no blaze to be seen. The blaze was in the chimney—only in the chimney. I closed the damper. Smoke billowed out into the room. Lucy appeared from nowhere. Our eyes blinked and smarted shut. We choked. We opened all the doors, and smoke, and heat, and Lucy, and I, rushed out of the place together.

We got the fire out too, at last. An hour later Lucy and I stood shivering again in our living room. It was as cold again as it had been the night before. It was dirty. It smelled. We were not happy. We put on our coats again, our hats, and mufflers, and mitts, and sat down to breakfast. The butter was a bit hard, and the toast was cold, but the bacon was very good.

# PART 15

## Such Goings On

*Let other vo'k meake money vaster*
*In the air o' dark-roomed towns,*
*I don't dread a peevish measter;*
*Though noo man do heed my frowns,*
*I be free to goo abrode,*
*Or teake agean my homeward road*
*To where vor me the apple tree*
*Do lean down low in Linden Lea.*

WILLIAM BARNES, 1800

# 43

## *We Dispose of Friends*

WINTER WAS HERSELF. MEDONTE WAS DECENTLY WHITE.
The hundred hills that fold down to Moonstone Creek
slept quietly under the deep snow that covered them.
Shining drifts buried the fences. The red-roofed range
shelters on the Owl Pen pasture field were lost completely.
Even Moonstone Creek itself was hidden. Our hills slept,
and our fields slept. There was neither movement nor
sound. The sun shone.

Even in the farm houses, the barnyards, and the woodlots, life moved slowly. In the farm houses the only sounds
to be heard between meal-times were the clump-bang of
wood being dropped into the wood box by the kitchen
stove, the rustle of mail order catalogues, and the click
of knitting needles. In the barns there was quiet, except

for the crunch-crunch of cattle chewing cud, or the suck and scamper of little pigs, and the sleepy grunting of their patient dams. The woodlots were utterly still.

Such peace, they say on our concession line, is "agin all nature". They call such calm and golden days "weather-breeders". They don't like them. "Too good to last," they say. They find a thousand signs to prove that settled winter weather, with sun-filled days, and clear, frosty nights, is just a calm before a mighty change that will unsettle everything.

"It's coming," warned Farmer Jim one night when we went uphill to Plum Tree Farm for our milk. "It's coming, sure as sin. The cattle are getting restless. T'other day I had to chase them out of the barn to water. Tonight I had to put the dog on them to get them in. The old sow's barking. The horses are stamping in their stalls. Everything's restless.

"You think . . . ?" I began.

"I know it," said Jim. "We're heading for our January thaw."

Lucy and I weren't so sure. It was true that the wind cowl on the brooder house ventilator had swung from the northwest, to which it had been pointing steadily for weeks, to the southeast, but we had seen it swing southeast before, and nothing had come of it, except a bit of snow. Still, the snow was rather packy underfoot. There were mice tracks and squirrel tracks in the snow by the creek, and Skudger, our tom cat, had been yowling in a way that he had never yowled before. We had even seen a crow.

"Could be," I agreed, uncertainly.

"Could be," grinned Lucy, and held out her hand to a tiny spatter of rain.

The January thaw was indeed upon us. The last sound that Lucy and I heard that night was the tap-tap-tap of rain drops on the roof above our bed. The first sound we heard in the morning was the crinkle and crash of icicles falling from the Owl Pen eaves. We got up to find long-buried fences showing through the snow on the side hill. We could even see spots of red in our pasture field where the roofs of our range shelters were lifting through the shrinking drifts. The world was filled with the small, clear, bell-like tinkling of melting snow. A muffled roaring came from the ice-shrouded spillway of the dam. A widening stain of pale gray-green on the snow of the valley told of rising waters in Moonstone Creek.

Our days of peace, and quietude, were finished. Peace flees the concession lines when snow begins to melt. It flees the farm house kitchen, and when the farmer seeks it in his barn, he finds that it had fled that place, too. There is no peace to be had sitting in a cow byre staring at mountains of turnips, wondering if the mild weather is going to last long enough to start them sprouting, and spoiling. There is no peace to be had watching rows of hung-up cabbages—that were meant for chicken feed—blacken and drip. There is no peace to be had where every living thing is snorting and stamping and shoving about in its pen or stall, yanking at its tie rope, pulling at its chain, dreaming of spring. On the first day of a January thaw it is a wise farmer who has brains enough to take his gun down from the kitchen wall and high-tail it for the bush.

If I had been possessed of enough sense to do just that, we at Owl Pen might still be the proud owners of two milkless milk goats, Suzanne and Josephine. They might still be lifting their funny faces in our now empty goat pen to bid us good morning and good night. But no, I hadn't enough sense to make myself scarce. I stayed around home, and got myself involved once again in the cleaning of stove pipes. It wasn't that we fought this time. We were determined to avoid that. We "darlinged" and

"deared" each other until we were sick of the sound of
the words.

"Darling, please, you're getting soot all over my clean
floor!"

"I wish you'd hold this d-d-difficult pipe a little steadier,
DEAR!"

"Yes, DARLING!"

"Yes, DEAR!"

When the messy job was finished and Lucy had blud-
geoned me with a last "darling" and I had knifed her with
a last "dear" I went out to the goat pen to rest my troubled
soul among duck-quacks and goat-bleats. I opened the
door of the goat pen to find Sue out of her stall and
standing, goggle-eyed and sway-backed, by the grain bin.
She was packed to the gunwales with oats. I put her
back in her stall, and tied her there, and went back to
the house.

"Sue jumped her stall," I told Lucy.

"How about some wood?" said she.

I got the wood and went back to the goat pen again.
Jo was out this time, stamping kittenishly about on the
milk stand, with her forefeet in a half-filled egg basket,
and with egg yolk on her chin. I counted ten—slowly, and
put her back where she belonged. I knew what she was
looking for, but I had no sympathy for her. Even a nanny
goat should have enough brains to know that an egg basket is the last place on earth to look for a billy goat.

Back to the house I went again.

"Jo has smashed our eggs," I wailed.

"How about fixing the meat?" Lucy wanted to know.

While I took our thaw-threatened meat supply out of
the storage shed and packed it in barrels of snow, I thought
the matter over. I brooded glumly. Those goats had
always been trouble makers. They had always been breachy.
Man had not yet invented the fence they could not pass.

They had driven us crazy all summer and fall. Now they were jumping their stall, raiding grain bins, smashing eggs, getting all ready to drive us crazy again. They were dry. They were useless. I marched up the hill to the house.

"The time has come for us to be practical," I told Lucy. "Those goats are fat . . . "

"You mean . . . " she broke in, a green light of foreboding flaring in her eyes. "You mean . . . ?"

"I mean that we have a big dog that is costing us a fortune to feed. Those goats won't feed us—dry as chips —have been for months—will be for months." I saw Lucy's lips grow thin, but I hurried on with what I had to say. "They are eating us out of house and home, and giving us nothing in return. That isn't practical. We'll have to buy more hay in a day or so. We are running short of straw. I could use their stall for the geese."

"Well?" said Lucy.

"Well, I know a man who will come and take them away, and bring us back the meat and the hides. Those goats have lovely hides. The meat would feed Thunder the rest of the winter. The hides would look nice on our bedroom floor." Some last vestige of common sense warned me to shut up, to say no more.

"Our Jo," said Lucy, after a long pause.

"Yes."

"Our Sue."

"Yes."

"You Judas, you!" said Lucy and stamped away into the kitchen, slamming the door shut behind her.

"Who's a Judas?" I shouted after her, but she didn't hear me, and it didn't matter, for she would not have answered if she had.

She didn't need to. I knew the answer. But, dash it all, a man had to be practical. If every farmer was as silly about his stock as we were being the world would starve to death. The world would be piled two deep all over with cows, and sheep, and pigs, and under them all would be the bleached, starved bones of their erstwhile owners. Sheep were born to be mutton. Cows were born to be beef. Pigs were born to be pork. And goats, our Jo and Sue, were born to be . . . to be . . . to be . . .

I took off my rubber boots and pounded upstairs to the telephone. My mind was made up. I knew what I was going to do. I knew the number I wanted. I picked up the receiver.

"Give me . . . " I began, and heard Lucy come quietly to the foot of the stairs. "Give me . . . "

I couldn't say it, not with a photograph of Jo and Sue lying, quite by chance, on the desk beside me, not with Lucy standing at the foot of the stairs. "Give me long distance," I shouted.

I had remembered that an old friend that I had not seen for many years was farming in the Markham area. He had been an artist, still was for all I knew. But he was a farmer too, and being an artist turned farmer, a farmer-artist no less, he might have a soft spot in his heart for goats. He might. In a few minutes I had him on the other end of the line. Had him was the word for it.

"Hello, Johnnie."

"Hello, Ken."

I got right to the point. "Johnnie," I told him, "I have two fine goats here . . . lovely goats . . . big black and white ones. What kind? They are a rare cross between pure-bred Toggenburg and pure-bred French Alpine. Mongrel? No! No! They are a pure-bred mixture. They are dry now, but ready for breeding. I want to give them to you. I have no billy. You keep them. You breed them. You'll love them. Why do I want to give them to you? Well . . . Well . . . It is a rather personal sort of matter.

I'm sending them to you on the next train. Good-bye, Johnnie, good-bye."

Johnnie was still talking when I hung up. I couldn't quite make out what he was saying. I didn't want to. I was afraid to. I had found our goats a good home. Our lovely little milkless, fence jumping, pen jumping, oat guzzling, egg eating nannies were going away. I wasn't taking a chance of spoiling things by either hearing, or saying too much. I called a trucker, and went downstairs again. Lucy had tea ready. My favourite sandwiches were piled on the tea table.

"Silly, aren't we?" said Lucy.

I looked at her eyes, and smile, and I didn't think so.

# 44

*We Are Marooned*

IT IS HARD TO THINK OF A WORLD SO SMALL THAT THE
pole about which it revolves is the handle of a pump.
But that is the world to Medonte when the wind howls
out of the north, and all the snow on all the hills comes
down to lie in great drifts on the concession lines. Our
world grows small. It shrinks as the drifts grow, until,
if the storm lasts long enough, it is no bigger than a barnyard.

At Owl Pen our world grew just that small. The thaw
ended. Winter came back with a swoosh and a roar. Lucy
and I climbed out of bed to find that our old timber house
had become an island. On all sides of us, rolling in un-
broken miles of whiteness over all our horizons spread a
limitless sea of snow. The fences were buried again. The
concession was lost again. Had we a car, it would have
been useless to use. Had we horses, we would not have
been unkind enough to put them through such drifts. We
had skis, but no ski poles, and no ski harness. We were
marooned. Our world was bounded by a kitchen door,
our woodpile, and our chicken house. We quoted Cowper
on the solitude of Robinson Crusoe:

> *"I am monarch of all I survey:*
> *My right there is none to dispute:*
> *From the centre all round to the sea*
> *I am lord of the fowl and the brute . . ."*

Through the snow-spattered panes of our living room
window, we surveyed our kingdom. The storm had blown

itself out during the night. The dawn rose clear. The eastern horizon was a wild blaze of purple, and red, and gold. The long light streaked between the elm trees, painting miles of drifted snow with all the rainbow colours of the sky. Our lonely mailbox, standing forlornly by the trackless concession line, was bathed in a rosy glow. Our chicken house loomed grandly among wind-sculptured hummocks of purple and gold. A fine mist of tiny ice particles rained like a shower of diamonds out of the clear sky. No king in ancient Babylon, we told ourselves, had half so much beauty at his command as had we in our four-acre kingdom by Moonstone Creek.

But morning in the country is no time to stand dreaming by a frosted window pane. A king, even on Moonstone Creek, is not without responsibility to his subjects. I hung up my crown in the clothes closet and took out my parka and mitts. My minions were waiting for me in the chicken house—sixty chickens, seven roosters, five geese, and ten ducks. While I held court there beside the feed bins, with an upturned mash bucket as my throne, Lucy would hold sway in the kitchen, with her faithful retainers, Thunder, our pup, and Titch, Skudger, and Bumps, our cats.

I opened the door, and climbed out over the four feet of snow that the wind had piled against it. It seemed a shame to mark the lovely whiteness of the hillside with my lumbering feet, but there was no way of avoiding it. I wallowed waist deep, chin deep; I tripped and floundered and sank in the beautiful stuff, and came up shouting. I passed the pump, which showed only the tip of its upraised handle. Snow which had gotten under my collar melted on my neck and ran down over my stomach into my rubber boots.

Of course a great drift had grown over the chicken house door. There are times in the country when ordinarily patient farmers can be heard two miles telling the world

about drifts and doors. I dug down through the snow
to the latch and pulled. The door didn't open. I heaved
and kicked. Still the door didn't open. My subjects within,
aroused by the clamour, quacked, honked, clucked, and
crowed, yelling for breakfast, demanding food. I looked
around for the shovel, and saw it at last, a dim spot in the
distance, standing coyly by the Owl Pen door.

It had been twenty degrees below zero during the night.
It was still cold, and my feet were wet. I got the shovel.
I dug. I dug fast. When I finally stumbled into the comparative warmth of the chicken house, Drinkwater, our
little Mallard drake, flew four feet into the air. He was
that glad to see me, or the mash bucket in my hand. Vankleek, our prize Rouen drake, reared himself up on to his
fat back end and flapped his wings so enthusiastically as
to send his two brown wives sprawling headlong across
the pen floor. It was a nice gesture of homage, I thought.
In a third pen our third drake expressed his feeling of
exuberance at my entry by saying, quite simply "pfut!"

The man who doesn't think that fowls make satisfactory
subjects does not deserve to be a king, not even of a desert
island, not even of a storm-bound farm. No great warrior
of old was ever more grateful for a knighthood conferred
on him by a gartered emperor in a plush-lined hall of state
than were our ducks for the mash and oyster shell conferred on them by me that stormy morning in the chicken
house by Moonstone Creek. No king was ever more appreciative of the gratitude of a subject than was I when
Dirty Back, our pet pullet, hopped singing to my shoulder,
as I knelt to fill the iron feed troughs in the pullets' section of the building. Her gratitude, and that of her sisters,
made me almost forget the wet shirt that pressed my
stomach, and the ice water in my boots.

Of our geese, the less said the better. They were, as
usual, radicals, communists every one, to the very core of

their mean and nasty skulls. When I carried my mash buckets in to them, they did not cheer. They did not sing. They did not belt their wives, or even "pfut". They hissed. They came at me with outstretched necks and gaping bills, with hate in their eyes. I filled their mash bowls for them. I broke the ice out of their water pails, and put fresh water in. I gave them an armful of clover hay, and a handful of ground grit.

"Yah!" they said. "Yah! Hiss! Yah!"

"Yah!" said I.

Back at the Owl Pen the situation was more in hand. Even Robinson Crusoe would have appreciated and approved the picture there. The hearth was blazing. Breakfast was ready. Lucy was seated at her end of the table. My chair was ready at mine. In a solemn row on the old-fashioned sofa that flanks our table sat our three cats, their six green eyes fixed in an unwavering stare on the cream jug, their three tails twitching as one. Mother, son and little brother, they sat there, with their three chins just touching the edge of the table cloth.

On the other side of the table, perched bolt upright in the big easy chair, sat Thunder, our Great Dane. He towered head and shoulders above Lucy. He looked down on her. He looked down on the cats. He looked down on the cream jug too, but most especially did he look down on the brimming honey pot that stood beside it. His tail wagged slowly. One ear was permanently cocked.

So we breakfasted the morning after the big storm, and so we breakfasted every morning for days afterwards. For nearly a fortnight no wheel moved on our concession. No farmer found it wise, or necessary, to put his horses through the big drifts that filled the hollow by the creek. No mail came to our mail box. We had no visitors at all, except a wolf that tried hard one night to get into our chicken house.

# 45

## *We Admire a Pig*

THE STORY OF HERCULES, THE LITTLE PIG THAT WOULDN'T die, began, so far as Lucy and I were concerned, the night we stumbled off the drifted concession line, with our milk pails and lantern, into the lamp-lit warmness of the kitchen at Plum Tree Farm. We heard strange sounds as we stood in the wood shed, brushing the snow from our backs and boots. We heard sweet music as we opened the kitchen door, familiar music in the late winter time in a Medonte farm house kitchen—the scamper, squeal, and scrutter of baby pigs.

"Gertrude's?" we asked, naming Jim's big sow, an especial favourite of ours.

"Not this time," said Jim, closing the mail order catalogue that was spread on his knees, and picking up his pipe. "They had a litter of fifteen down at dad's place the other day. Too many for one sow this kind of weather. We got five to bring up by hand."

"Think we'll do it?" asked Alice.

"You have before," said Lucy.

We peeled back the rag rug covering the big box by the wood stove and looked in. The five baby pigs were quiet again, nestled together in a small, tangled heap of satiny wee bodies. They were as pinkly naked as human babies, and much smaller, less than a foot long, less than six inches high.

"It's hard to imagine such dainty little things growing in six months' time into great hulking brutes, weighing nearly three hundred pounds . . . " I exclaimed.

"With nasty big tusks," put in Lucy.

"And strong enough to kill a horse," I finished.

"I hope they are," sighed Jim.

"They look all right," I protested, catching a note of despair in Jim's voice. "They are quiet and contented . . . "

"They are too quiet," said Farmer Jim.

The next night there were only three little pigs in the box by the wood stove at Plum Tree Farm. Two little bodies lay in the snow back of the barn. Another day passed and another piglet died. When the morning of the third day dawned a fourth little pig lay dead in the box, and the one survivor, Hercules himself, lay on his side, groaning and kicking, his eyes glazed, his mouth open.

"He's a gonner," said Alice.

"Mebbe," said Jim, and picked the little fellow out of the box.

"What are you going to do?"

"I'm going to doctor him," announced Jim. "I don't rightly know what the matter is. I've an idea, that's all. I don't rightly know what should be done, but I'm going to do something. It's kill or cure. If I leave him alone, he'll die anyway."

Jim's first thought was of turpentine, the old standby on the concession line. Good for shoe polish, and good for paint, it is good too, according to a dozen generations of farmers, for any number of things that go wrong with a horse, or a cow, or a pig. It drives out worms. It raises blisters. It helps a sore throat. It cleans a wound. Jim looked where the turpentine was usually kept and found none. He did find some coal oil.

"So I gave him some of that," said Jim, "a good swig."

An hour passed, or maybe two, and the little pig didn't seem any better. As a matter of fact, it seemed a lot worse. The stuff that makes lamp light seemed to be putting the little pig's light out entirely. Its jaws were working. Its eyes were closed. It groaned weakly. Had Jim been a medical man attending a human being, he might well have told somebody to call the undertaker. Instead, he gave the patient a big spoonful of castor oil.

Strangely enough, the little pig did not seem to like the castor oil any better than it did the coal oil. It frothed at the mouth. It kicked spasmodically, and then grew rigid. It seemed as good as dead. Farmer Jim picked it out of the box again and rubbed its poor little tummy. What to do? What to do? There was no use calling a veterinary. The roads were blocked with six foot drifts of crusted snow. Not even a horse could get through them. Maybe the little beast had gas on its stomach.

"I remembered some stuff that I had in the barn," said Jim, "stuff that I had got for a horse that was bloated. Of course there is a lot of difference between a big work horse and a baby pig, but there didn't seem much point in not trying the stuff."

The little pig still groaned.

Later in the day Jim came upon another bottle, a big flask that had contained a patent stock medicine. The stuff had been long unused and had dried up. The bottle was empty except for a thick, purple crust in the bottom. It didn't look very nice, and when he had added a bit of pump water, and shaken it up, it didn't smell very nice. Still, it was medicine, bought'n medicine, too. Jim went back into the farm house kitchen.

The baby pig was past protesting. It took what was given it now, without a struggle, without a cry. The mauve nastiness gurgled in the poor thing's limp and flabby throat. Looking at it sprawled helplessly in the bottom of the box by the wood stove, Jim decided that it was not long for this world, that it was a matter of minutes only, or of an hour at most, before it joined its brothers and sisters in that golden sty beyond the moon to which all good piglets go.

"If only I had some turpentine," he told himself. "I might have saved the little brute if I had been able to give it some of that. Turpentine is the stuff. I was sure I had some. There was a bottle . . . by golly, I know where it is!"

Down the wee pig's gullet ran a stream of turpentine, the crude, yellow, biting stuff that comes from a hardware store. The poor little beast, not more than a few days' old, and weighing not over a pound and a half, had survived coal oil, and castor oil, and two kinds of patent medicine. Now to the miseries inflicted upon it by these, and by its original ailment, was being added a generous helping of that stinging spirit which is usually used to thin paint.

"No use hanging around," decided Jim. "I've done what I can. It will live or it will die."

Of course, it should have died. Jim came back from the barn a while later expecting to find it dead. He didn't. The little thing was on its feet. Its eyes were open. It wasn't shuddering any more. It wasn't groaning. It was yelling for food. Jim fed it. It slept an hour, and then yelled again for food. Alice was up twice in the night to feed it warm milk and corn syrup in order to keep it quiet.

"It's eating its head off," she told Lucy. "I never saw a baby pig eat like it. We just can't keep it filled up."

So Lucy and I now call the little pig at Plum Tree Farm by the fancy name of Hercules. Hercules, we maintain, is none too good a name for it, even though we have found out that Hercules will grow up to be a sow. Any little pig that lives through what that piglet lived through deserves the best. Nobody around here can guess why she didn't die. Lucy and I can't figure it out. Jim can't. Alice can't. It should have died of the coal oil, say some. Others insist that it was the coal oil that saved it, and that it was the castor oil that might have finished it off. Some think that the patent medicines staved off both the coal oil and the castor oil, and gave the turpentine a chance to work. Farmer Jim inclines to this latter theory.

"Turps is good stuff," he says.

We all agree on one point only—that it should have died. It didn't.

Viva Hercules!

# PART 16

## Eden Is Four Acres

*"Our dreams are all we own."*

OWL PEN HEARTHSTONE.

# 46

## *We See Signs of Spring*

CALENDARS DON'T COUNT. DATES DON'T MATTER. NEITHER do the drifts that still block our concession lines, or the thermometer in the Owl Pen doorway which says that, out of the sun, it is nearly zero. What does matter is that, in the sun, the snow is melting, disintegrating with a clear, bell-like tinkling that is lovely music in a winter-weary farmer's ears. Great clouds of steam are drifting from the south side of every barn roof in the township. The manure piles are smoking. The sun is growing warmer. Spring is just over the hill.

It may be a high hill. We in Medonte will grant that. It may be a time coming. We will go that far with a cynic. But spring is on her way just the same. There are signs all around to point this fact, signs that the stupidly learned meteorologists and almanac makers, will never understand. There is the goose egg that Lucy and I found in the goose pen the other day. There are those queer little marks in the snow along Moonstone Creek, marks that weren't there yesterday, or the day before yesterday.

Upstream from the old cattle bridge, the marks in the snow tell clearly of a big raccoon that dabbled where the water runs fast between big stones and doesn't freeze. Now a raccoon doesn't like winter. It sleeps through the most of it, denned up in a hollow tree, or in an old straw stack, and only comes out when it has reason to believe that the worst of the bad weather is past. When a farmer sees 'coon tracks in a snowbank, he begins looking at his sap pails. Spring isn't far off. You can't fool a 'coon.

Just back of the barn on Green Shadows Farm there is another spot where Moonstone Creek doesn't freeze. There are marks in the snow on the banks there too, little rows of dots that go clippity-clip, clippity-clip through the cedars. They are skunk tracks, neat little foot prints made by a fellow who doesn't like winter any more than a raccoon does. You can see where he has dug into the top of a rotten stump, looking for hibernating beetles, and further down stream you can see where he has been feasting on the head of a steer that was killed for winter meat. When a man in Medonte sees skunk tracks, he begins thinking about new plough points. He telephones his implement dealer. A skunk can smell spring a mile off. You can't fool a skunk.

If a man doesn't like to believe the writing in the snow, he can look up and read the same message written in the tree branches. He will see that the buds on every tree are swollen—not so big and red as they will be in a few weeks' time, but bigger and redder than they were a few weeks ago. If he doesn't know what that means, he is not as wise as the squirrels.

A week or two ago, there was hardly a squirrel to be seen in the bushlots. Now they are all over the place. The tree tops are spotted with them. In every other beech or birch tree especially, there is a red squirrel swinging, or a black squirrel, or a gray. They are eating the buds, filling up on buds. Their winter stores are forgotten. When a squirrel sinks his long yellow teeth into a beech bud, and finds that the sun has been warm enough to fill it with life and sweetness, it knows that spring is on the way. The mere fact that the thermometer still registers zero, or thereabouts, doesn't mean a thing. You can't fool a squirrel.

Yet still Lucy and I were hard to convince. We saw the marks in the snow, both up creek and down. We saw the buds in the trees, and squirrels of three colours eating them. We saw our neighbours checking their sap buckets, and polishing plough points. We saw, too, the drifts on the concession line, and the shriveled-up bit of mercury in the bottom of the thermometer tube. They are all crazy, we decided, raccoons and neighbours, skunks, squirrels, and buds. We were not at all inclined to either feel, or admit, that spring was in the air.

"It's unreasonable," said Lucy.

"Unseasonable," said I.

Even when we tripped, three days running, over unheeding pullets that crowded by the door in the chicken house that separated them from the cockerels, we thought nothing of it. We watched our pretty Mallard and Rouen drakes bobbing their silly mating dance around their stolid wives, and that didn't mean anything to us. (It didn't seem to mean much to their wives, either.) We noticed that a bright red blush was growing on the pale orange beaks of our gray geese, and still we weren't impressed.

We didn't notice, so blind were we to the significance of it all, that one of our geese had laid a huge white egg on the one bare spot of cement floor in their straw-littered pen. Our reason told us that a goose egg in February, and a cold February at that, was most unlikely, if not impossible. Common-sense closed our eyes to the obvious. Not until it had lain on the floor for a day and a half did we put reason by and open our eyes and ears to what every bird and beast in the township had been shouting for a week. We saw the egg.

It was frozen when we found it, frozen and cracked. Our first goose egg was lost to us, simply because we had too many brains to take a skunk seriously, simply because we had been too impressed by calendars and thermometers to admit the weather-wisdom of a 'coon, simply because we had preferred to listen to the learned silliness of meteorologists, instead of the wiser hissing of our own gray geese. I carried the big egg across the drifted pasture field into the Owl Pen, and laid it on the living room table.

"It should have been our first gosling," I told Lucy. "I should have seen it, but I was so sure that it would be weeks before our geese started laying . . . the books all say that a goose won't start laying until spring is . . . "

"It seems that spring is," said Lucy, weighing the great egg in her two hands. "Poor little unborn gosling," she murmured, and then, just to rub it in, "we're murderers, you know."

It's wonderful the changes a frozen goose egg can work in the life of a man and a woman. Until that egg arrived, there was peace at Owl Pen, the deep peace, and utter quietude of long winter days, and longer winter nights. Lucy and I did our chores in a leisurely fashion, stretching them out with minutes spent leaning indolently over the duck pen railings, chatting with Drinkwater, our Mallard drake, and with Vankleek, our Rouen. We squatted, half an hour at a time, in the chicken pen, gossiping with Dirty Back, our pet pullet, and with Beefy, our pet rooster.

There was no reason to hurry. Our books were never the worse for waiting an hour or two unread. And Thunder had a way of keeping the big easy chair by the fireplace warm, while we were out of the house. Spring was a long way off, we told ourselves. There is no need to rush the setting of nests in the duck pen, or goose pen. There was lots of time in which to make the brooder house ready for the baby chicks we had ordered. There was lots of time for everything, we thought, as we looked at the drifted concession line. Lots of time . . . lots of time . . .

And then the egg arrived.

The other day a frost-filled wind whined out of the north, driving the snow from all the surrounding hills down into our valley, driving it in a great, swirling fog across our pasture field. Through it all staggered Lucy and I. A four-foot drift grew in front of the brooder house. We burrowed through it, carrying coal and sand, and newly disinfected feed troughs, making all ready for the baby chicks so soon to be ours. Ice froze the padlock on the storage shed door into an immoveable mass. We got hot water, and thawed it out. There were boxes in the shed that we needed as nests for our ducks. Spring was on its way. We were convinced of that at last. Our goose had laid an egg. You can't fool a goose. Every hour, on the hour, from dawn until sunset, we wallowed back and forth across the drifted field between the Owl Pen and the goose pen.

"Can't take a chance of another egg freezing," we gasped each time we returned, empty handed, to our fireside. "Can't take a chance."

We got a second egg, eventually, and then a third, and a fourth, and then a bad cold.

Sprig is cubbig.

Sniff! Sniff!

Can't fool us.

# 47

## *We Learn About Roosters*

UNTIL QUITE RECENTLY WE HAD THREE ROOSTERS AT OWL
Pen. Every morning, all winter long, as the rosy-fingered
dawn painted the snow on the eastern hills with the first
light of a new day, their wild, clear bugle song rang out over
Moonstone Creek. It rang from that part of the Owl
Pen chicken house which was sacred to the bachelorhood
of the three cockerels we were keeping separate from the
pullets until spring made it reasonable for fowls to think
of romance. It rang from the throats of three finely-
feathered musketeers of the spur who had never quarrelled,
and who, we fondly believed, never would.

Lucy and I were proud of our three roosters. They were
the pick of the flock that had grown out of the three hundred baby chicks that we had brought to Owl Pen on
a hand sleigh over the drifted roads of last March. They
had survived our bungling. They had resisted the multitude of diseases that had afflicted, and destroyed, many
of their brothers and sisters. They were fine birds, gloriously
white, with crimson faces, golden beaks, and legs that shone
like the sun. They were sturdy, healthy, and arrogant.
They walked sideways, on tip-toe, like boxers in a ring.
They were, in short, three perfect answers to a pullet's
dream.

There was Long John, a phlegmatic sort of fellow, a
bit too upright in carriage to please an expert's eye, but
stout of bone, and big of heart, a heavy, easy-going sort
of bird that nothing seemed to excite or upset. He was
always giving way to the other two roosters that shared

the pen with him. It wasn't that they bullied him. Not
that. It was just his nature to let them have the choice
of the roosting places, and placidly to make do with what
was left. If they wanted his place at the feed trough, or
at the water pail, they took it. John didn't mind. There
were other places just as good. On more than one ocasion,
Lucy and I watched him call his companions over to his
side of the cock pen to share with him a particularly fine
morsel of caked mash that he had found. John was like
that. There was nothing mean or nasty about John.

Bubbling Pete was quite a different type of lad. He
was an under-slung sort of fellow, low-down and drawn-
out. We had kept him as an answer to Long John's
uprightness. Pete was self-seeking. He was selfish. He
shared nothing with anybody. He gave way to nobody. He
was boss of the pen. He said so, and the others didn't
bother to argue the point—Long John, because the point
was, very apparently, of little importance to him, and
Goops, the third rooster, because argument did not sort
well with his way of getting along in the world.

Goops was an opportunist, a politician. He was just
what might have been expected of a bird with such a
name. He was fat-headed and heavy jowled. He was
dignified, in a slippery sort of way. His side was the win-
ning side—always. He was always with Long John, when
Long John happened to find something interesting in the
straw that littered the pen floor. He was always with
Bubbling Pete when Pete happened to be the lucky one.
The few times that Lucy or I ever saw him alone in the
pen, he was in the exact centre of it, poised in an agony
of indecision, unable to decide whether it would be most
advantageous for him to join Pete at the grain feeder, or
Long John at the mash trough. Goops should have been
born under a wet plank. He was that sort of fellow.

Perhaps it was because of, and not in spite of, the differences in their characters and personalities that our birds got along so well together. They saw the winter through without a single quarrel. No spur was ever lifted in anger, not real anger, by an Owl Pen rooster against an Owl Pen rooster. There may have been a bit of pushing at times, especially around the narrow crack under the door that separated the roosters from the pullets, but that was always the pullets' fault. They kept sticking their pretty beaks through the crack (the shameless hussies) egging our roosters on.

At last the day dawned when Owl Pen plans ordained that something beautiful should happen in the lives of Long John, Bubbling Pete and even Goops, the politician. Twenty of our best layers were to be given them, for better or for worse, until practical considerations did them part again. Lucy and I took our poultry books out to the chicken house. We pinned our pictures of ideal, and prize-winning Chanticlers to the chicken house wall, and then we turned to the brides to be.

We had to be careful. We were establishing our breeding flock. Mistakes made now would have their effect on generations yet unborn. The pullets we chose had to be the best in our laying pen. We looked them over. This one we chose because she had a broad back, indicating good laying capacity, and a bright eye, indicating vigour. This one we rejected because she had the wrong kind of comb. This one we argued over because she was perfect except for an item which I thought inconsequential, and which Lucy thought was important. Only Dirty Back, our pet, passed through our hands without hesitation, and without discussion. As a friend, she was beyond criticism. We tossed her into the cock pen, with the pious hope that she would like what she found there.

There was no doubt left in the mind of any living thing at Owl Pen that day as to the reactions of the three mus-

keteers to the company that was being given them. Even
our ducks stopped their gabbling to listen to it. Our
stately gray Canada geese stood like graven images, their
eyes popping with utter amazement at such goings on.
Pandemonium, bedlam, filled the chicken house. Squk,
and caw, and chortle, and crow, was just a small part of
it. Lucy and I stopped work, and went into the cock pen
to see for ourselves the reason for such a din.

"I've seen all this before," said Lucy, after we had
watched the show for a few minutes, "and it wasn't in a
chicken house."

I don't think that we will ever enjoy eating chicken
again. Chickens are too human. Or humans are too
chicken-like. We watched Long John prance side-ways
up to a pullet that took his fancy. We watched the pullet
do everything but wink. And then, bingo, we watched
Bubbling Pete charge in. We watched John fly squawking
away from him. Pete gave chase. Round and round the
breeding pen went Long John, his eyes bulging with hor-
rified unbelief that a friend should treat him so, his beak
agape with protest. Round and round the breeding pen
after him went Pete, yelling bloodily of battle, and sudden death. We watched the two fools run themselves to
the point of exhaustion, and, as might be expected, we
watched Goops, the opportunist, the politician, walk off
with the girl.

So went the cock pen comedy for days, and then fate
decided that our roads should close with six foot drifts of
snow, and that I should walk over them six miles to post
a letter. I got to the distant highway to find a telephone
message awaiting me. I was to call home at once. There
was trouble at home. Terrible trouble.

"I don't know exactly what," my informant told me,
"your wife was too upset to speak plain. She did say something about blood. Maybe somebody is killed."

I called home. Lucy was excited. There had been a fight in the chicken house. The fight was still going on. Our three musketeers of the spur, our three friendly roosters, were tearing each other apart.

"They've gone crazy," whooped Lucy. "Our lovely looking roosters look awful now. What should I do? What can I do? Why do you have to be away at a time like this?"

I knew what had happened, or I thought I did. Pete had at last caught up with Long John. He had herded the poor, patient fellow into a corner, and there beaten and clawed him into a livid pulp. As a sort of after-thought, he had then proceeded to take Goops apart. The thought of Goops getting at last that which he should have got long ago rather pleased me, but the thought of poor old Long John being kicked about was rather upsetting.

"Put Pete in a feed bag," I told Lucy. "Keep him there until I get home. I'll settle his hash; we'll eat him."

"Me put that bloody, savage, fighting fool of a bird in a feed bag!" exclaimed Lucy.

"Yes."

"I'll try." The answer came in a still, small voice.

When I got home I went straight to the chicken house. Lucy was there, white of face, and quite unhappy. She hadn't been able to put Bubbling Pete in a bag. She hadn't been able to get him out of the nest in which he was hiding. I went into the cock pen. Pete was still in the nest, cowering and shuddering in the darkness over three trampled eggs. Goops I found huddled under the perches, his face a tattered, bloody mask. Long John, patient, long-suffering, gentle Long John, I found strutting unconcernedly among his twenty wives, HIS twenty wives, lord at last of the cock pen, master of all it contained.

I was tired after my trip, but I took off my hat to that

rooster. I got down on my knees and took him up in my arms.

"Cut-caw," he said quietly. "Cut-caw."

"You old hero," I whispered.

Long John looked me straight in the eye.

I think he winked.

# 48

*We End Our Book*

THE CREEK THAT RUNS PAST OWL PEN IS A VERY LITTLE creek. Though all the hills slant down to it, though it drains a valley that is many miles long, it is, except in flood time, a mere trickle of water with pools that are nowhere big enough, or deep enough, to shelter more than a trout. Minks and muskrats, foxes and raccoons are its constant companions. Occasionally a grave, gray heron visits it.

At this time of year the little creek is, for the most part, hidden under a deep mantle of snow. A wanderer might walk over it a dozen times, in a dozen different places, and not even guess that under his feet creek-water was laughing still. Only where small rapids prevent the ice from forming does the water show itself, and there the wanderer may pause, and think of spring, as he looks at water cress, still fresh and green despite freezing winds and drifting snow.

Perhaps this green water cress is the reason why Lucy and I find it hard to keep away from Moonstone Creek in the winter of the year. Somehow every walk we take ends by its side. Though we start uphill, our path curves despite us into a great wobbly half circle that brings us, willy-nilly, not to hill-top elms, and broad stone walls, but to creek-side thickets, and the glint of water. It is disconcerting. Still, green is a comfortable colour, the colour of hope. We like the look of those tufty heads of cress bobbing under the water, bobbing away from the snow-covered banks, bobbing "hello'.

Someday soon, Lucy and I intend to take another walk. We'll head straight for the creek-bank this time, straight for the freshet where the water cress grows. We have a little stock-taking to do, a little reviewing of our life together at Owl Pen, and it will be nice to have something fresh and green to look at while we do it. The colour of hope is important at times.

Keeping our eyes firmly fixed on the bronzy-green cress, we will take a long look back over our first year with chickens. We will remember the high hopes we had as we drew our first lot, three hundred wildly cheeping morsels of yellow fluff, home on a hand sleigh over the snow-drifted roads of last March. We will remember what happened in the brooder house, and what happened on the growing range, and what happened in the pullet house. We will think of them dying, by the dozen and by the score, and of the diseases that afflicted them, and of our own bungling.

Still keeping our eyes fixed on the bobbing water cress, we will next consider our ducks. We will remember the sunny day our twenty-five-day-old ducklings arrived by train from a distant breeder. We will remember our joy at the beauty of them. They were to be our breeding flock. They were supposed to be Rouen ducks, the most beautiful of all domestic ducks, and the finest fleshed. We will remember how they grew up to be feathered monstrosities, everything and anything except the Rouens of our books. They had not metallic green heads, no claret-coloured breasts, no French-blue bodies, no brick-red feet. They had black breasts and white wings. Some were actually striped, and still others developed great tufty top-knots of feathers on their heads.

We will consider our geese. I think that when Lucy and I come to this subject we will pick some of the water cress and hold it tightly in our hands. We had trouble with our geese too. We weren't to be satisfied with ordinary domestic geese. No, indeed no. We bought a pair of stately wild Canada geese. Aristrocrats of the northland, we called them when we saw them in their travelling crate at the Owl Pen door. Aristocrats they proved. Not for them the mundane chores of domesticity. The gander proved to be too proud to even kiss the goose, and the goose too haughty to lay.

It is only when we come to consider our bees that we will be able to safely take our eyes off the comforting greenness in the brook, and perhaps let fall the wilted sprigs in our hands. Last spring we knew nothing about bees. Our books advised us to start bee-keeping with no more than two colonies. We started with fifty. We should have been stung to death. We weren't. We should have lost our bees. We didn't. Instead, in a year of general crop failure, we reaped a moderately good crop of fine white honey. Where the experts failed, we succeeded. We did everything that we should not have done, and nothing that we should have done, and our bees loved it.

Fate is a clown, we have decided. Even with our goats he has been a funny man with us. We love him for it. The expected never happens at Owl Pen. The unexpected always does. We have worried, and despaired, and yet we would not have a single day of our life at Owl Pen changed. We have had fun. We have bought experience. We have learned a lot. We have a new lot of chicks coming. We have Rouen ducks now that are Rouen ducks. We have common, garden-variety gray geese that lay their heads off. Our bee-yards grow. Next year we will discover a thousand new ways of making a thousand new mistakes. And we will learn some more of what a man and a woman must learn who would live on a concession line.

We have our hawthorne bush.

PHOTOGRAPHS
TAKEN BY THE AUTHOR
AT THE OWL PEN